Christoper Dewangga Pramudita

The Balanced Scorecard as Strategic Controlling Instrument

Introducing the Indicators-based BSC for Implementation of a Corporate Strategy from Four Different Perspectives

Anchor Academic Publishing

Pramudita, Christoper Dewangga: The Balanced Scorecard as Strategic Controlling Instrument. Introducing the Indicators-based BSC for Implementation of a Corporate Strategy from Four Different Perspectives, Hamburg, Anchor Academic Publishing 2016

Buch-ISBN: 978-3-96067-041-4
PDF-eBook-ISBN: 978-3-96067-541-9
Druck/Herstellung: Anchor Academic Publishing, Hamburg, 2016

Bibliografische Information der Deutschen Nationalbibliothek:
Die Deutsche Nationalbibliothek verzeichnet diese Publikation in der Deutschen Nationalbibliografie; detaillierte bibliografische Daten sind im Internet über http://dnb.d-nb.de abrufbar.

Bibliographical Information of the German National Library:
The German National Library lists this publication in the German National Bibliography. Detailed bibliographic data can be found at: http://dnb.d-nb.de

All rights reserved. This publication may not be reproduced, stored in a retrieval system or transmitted, in any form or by any means, electronic, mechanical, photocopying, recording or otherwise, without the prior permission of the publishers.

Das Werk einschließlich aller seiner Teile ist urheberrechtlich geschützt. Jede Verwertung außerhalb der Grenzen des Urheberrechtsgesetzes ist ohne Zustimmung des Verlages unzulässig und strafbar. Dies gilt insbesondere für Vervielfältigungen, Übersetzungen, Mikroverfilmungen und die Einspeicherung und Bearbeitung in elektronischen Systemen.

Die Wiedergabe von Gebrauchsnamen, Handelsnamen, Warenbezeichnungen usw. in diesem Werk berechtigt auch ohne besondere Kennzeichnung nicht zu der Annahme, dass solche Namen im Sinne der Warenzeichen- und Markenschutz-Gesetzgebung als frei zu betrachten wären und daher von jedermann benutzt werden dürften.

Die Informationen in diesem Werk wurden mit Sorgfalt erarbeitet. Dennoch können Fehler nicht vollständig ausgeschlossen werden und die Diplomica Verlag GmbH, die Autoren oder Übersetzer übernehmen keine juristische Verantwortung oder irgendeine Haftung für evtl. verbliebene fehlerhafte Angaben und deren Folgen.

Alle Rechte vorbehalten

© Anchor Academic Publishing, Imprint der Diplomica Verlag GmbH
Hermannstal 119k, 22119 Hamburg
http://www.diplomica-verlag.de, Hamburg 2016
Printed in Germany

Table of contents

List of Figures

List of Tables

List of Symbols/Abbreviations

Chapter 1 Introduction 1

    1.1.   Problem Description 1

    1.2.   Objectives 3

    1.3.   Structure 4

Chapter 2 BSC as A Strategic Controlling Instrument 6

    2.1.   Traditional Performance Measurement Concepts as Predecessor of BSC 6

    2.2.   Comparing BSC with Traditional Performance Measurement 7

    2.3.   Controlling Instruments 8

    2.3.1.   Operational Instruments 8

    2.3.2.   Strategic instruments 9

    2.4.   Balanced Scorecard (BSC) 11

    2.4.1.   Implementation of BSC 13

    2.4.2.   Targets and tasks of BSC 17

    2.5.   The four-perspectives of BSC 18

    2.5.1.   Financial 20

    2.5.2.   Customer 21

    2.5.3.   Internal business process 21

    2.5.4.   Learning and growth 22

    2.6.   Strategic targets formulated in the four perspectives 23

    2.7.   The concept of indicators system 25

    2.7.1.   Monetary indicators 27

    2.7.2.   Non-monetary indicators 28

Chapter 3 Implementation of BSC in automobile industries 29

    3.1.   *BSC at Daimler AG* 29

    3.2.   *BSC at BMW Group* 39

Chapter 4 Analysis of using BSC 48

    4.1.   *Cause-and-effect correlations* 48

    4.2.   *Advantages and Disadvantages of BSC* 50

    4.3.   *Chances and challenges of implementing BSC* 52

Chapter 5 Conclusion 53

List of References 55

List of Figures

Figure 1: The Four Primary Management Functions.
Figure 2: Balanced Scorecard Illustrated as a Cockpit of an Airplane.
Figure 3: Matrices Used in the BSC.
Figure 4: Balanced Scorecard Strategic Perspectives
Figure 5: The Four Perspectives of BSC Illustrated as a Process of Planting an Apple Tree.
Figure 6: The Concept of Indicators System.
Figure 7: Product Portfolio of Daimler AG.
Figure 8: The Board of Management of Daimler AG.
Figure 9: ADAC Crash-test Brilliance BS6.
Figure 10: ADAC's Crash-test for Mercedes C-class.
Figure 11: Corporate Facts: Board of Management of BMW Group.
Figure 12: Five Years Summary of Non-financial and Financial Performance Indicators of BMW Group Showed in Column Charts.

List of Tables

Table 1: Five Years Summary of Daimler AG's Financial Report 2014.
Table 2: Five Years Summary of Non-financial Performance Indicators of BMW Group.
Table 3: Five Years Summary of Financial Performance Indicators of BMW Group.

List of Symbols/Abbreviations

AG	Aktiengesellschaft
BMW AG	Bayerische Motoren Werke Aktiengesellschaft
BSC	Balanced Scorecard
CEO	Chief Executive Officer
CF	Cash flow
e.g.	Exempli gratia/For example
EBIT	Earnings before Interest and Taxes
EBITDA	Earnings before Interest, Taxes, Depreciation and Amortization
EFQM	European Foundation for Quality Management
EVA	Economic Value Added
i.e.	id est/in other words/that is
p.a.	pro Annum/per year
R&D	Research and Development
ROA	Return on Asset
ROCE	Return on Capital Employed
ROE	Return on Equity
ROI	Return on Investment
ROS	Return on Sales
SAP SEM	SAP Strategic Enterprise Management
SAP	Systems, Applications & Products
SWOT	Strengths, Weakness, Opportunities and Threats
US	United States
USD	US Dollar
WC	Working Capital
ZVEI	Zentralverband der elektronischen Industrie

Chapter 1 Introduction

1.1. Problem Description

Nowadays, many companies should not only discuss about how to obtain profits from their products, which are successfully sold to their customers, but also they should be forced to use any other aspects that are able to give more impact for their long-term success. For examples, discussing about quality of their products, relationship between them and their customers and employees, and the production process as well as marketing. Those are the challenges for all managers who are not only struggling in achieving company's targets - high profits but also in achieving customer, employees and stakeholders satisfaction. Schermerhorn (2011, p. 16) generally sees the role of managers in a company and stated that all managers, regardless of their titles, levels, types, and organisational settings, are responsible for the four primary management functions which are defined by Lewis, et al. (2007) as planning, organising, leading, and controlling.

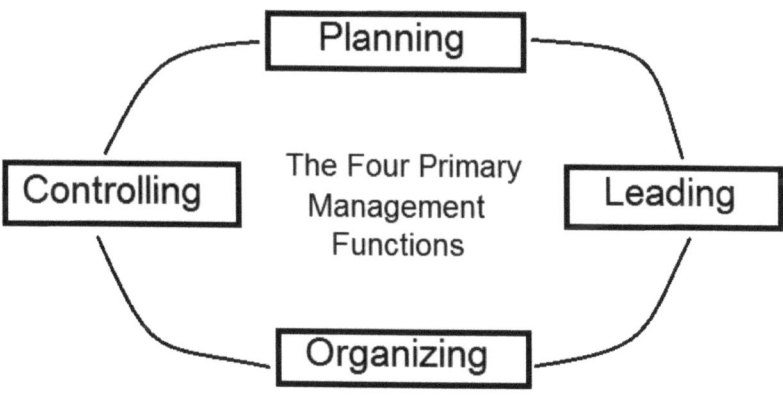

Figure 1 – The Four Primary Management Functions.
(Source: according to Lewis, et al. 2007)

a) **Planning** should be described that managers have tasks in setting targets and in defining actions that are necessary to achieve the targets of their companies.
b) **Organizing** involves determining the assignments to be done and how those assignments would be managed and coordinated to reach the company's targets.
c) **Leading** should be defined that managers should be able to guide, to motivate, and to lead the employees in order to effectively and efficiently achieve company's targets.
d) **Controlling** requires the managers to monitor process of planning, leading and organising whether its process may be able to help reaching the targets, targets have been achieved as expected and applied strategies have been effective or not.

It is difficult for managers to accept the challenges. Therefore, managers need to seek out an approach which is able to help them finishing their tasks and involves not only one aspect but any other aspects, such as customers, shareholders, internal business processes and employees. For other aspects, Tesarovicova (2008) clarified that a higher return on the funds and an increase of the company value is expected by shareholders and owners since customers expect a higher value and quality of products. Nevertheless, the problem appears where to reconcile conflicting demands of individual interest groups are not easy. She also argued that modern approaches are needed to be applied with an emphasis on their most important assets to the management of companies. In addition, the concept of balanced scorecard (BSC) is one of modern approaches that she mentioned.

To further understand about balanced scorecard, Averson (1998) issued an argument that the balanced scorecard is not only giving an alternative to the traditional financial key figures, but also it may give a description as well as explanation of what should be measured in order to assess whether applied strategies have been effective or not.

Not only Averson (1998) has argued regarding balanced scorecard, but Kaplan and Norton (1996, p. 7) also have argued that:

"The balanced scorecard retains traditional financial measures. But financial measures tell the story of past events, an adequate story for industrial age companies for which investments in long-term capabilities and customer relationships were not critical for success. These financial measures are inadequate, however, for guiding and evaluating the journey that information age companies must make to create future value through investment in customers, suppliers, employees, processes, technology, and innovation".

There is another opinion regarding balanced scorecard from Asefaso (2013). He argued that it enables executives to implement their strategies for real. He also stated that the balanced scorecard method gives a clear prescription as to what organisations should indicate in order to "balance" the financial perspective. Balanced scorecard itself is applied with the help of indicators system. Nevertheless, Poureisa, Ahmadgourabi and Efteghar (2013) stated that performance of indicators system has dramatically changed compared to the prior indicators. They argued that the indicator results are real when the comparisons are used between similar items. Based on traditional performance indicator method, they argued that the most significant targets of evaluation are performance indicators while modern method has focused on evaluated growth and development capacity. In other words, modern method should answer the questions. For examples, whether our customers are satisfied with our products, whether our employees have been very well treated and whether our production process has been efficient so that it increases our growth and development capacity, while the traditional performance indicators method focus on finance indicator such as Return on Investment (ROI), Return on Capital Employed (ROCE), Earnings Before Interest and Taxes (EBIT), Earnings Before Interest, Taxes, Depreciation and Amortization (EBITDA), Profitability, Revenue, and other indicators.

1.2. Objectives

According to Asefaso (2013), the balanced scorecard has developed from its early use as an easy performance indicator framework to a complete strategic planning as well as management system. It provides a framework that is not only provides performance indicators, but also gives a help for the planners to recognise what should be done and measured. Due to a complete tool for manager to navigate the successful of the company, BSC would be thoroughly reviewed through some examples of two German companies. The targets of this thesis are answering questions, for examples:

- Whether BSC may help managers to achieve the challenges which are described in the problem description.
- Whether it is true that BSC as strategic controlling instrument should be defined as a complete method which should increase performance of a company through its four different perspectives.
- Whether the positive impact of BSC usage may be clearly seen on the financial statement of company.
- Whether each company should pass the four different perspectives in implementing of BSC.

1.3. Structure

The main topic of this book is the balanced scorecard. However, it would be more specifically explained about the benefits of introducing the indicators-based balanced scorecard as a strategic controlling instrument for implementation of corporate strategy from four different perspectives. Before the conclusion, this thesis would be started from chapter 1 which is an introduction which would involve the problem description, the targets and the structure of this thesis. In this section, the challenges for the managers to manage their primary tasks and to achieve company goals linked to other aspects are introduced. Thus, chapter 1 contains problems which should be solved in the next chapter.

Chapter 2 would explain the theories about BSC as a strategic controlling instrument. It would also introduce the concept of BSC to solve the problems which are previously described in chapter 1. In addition, how BSC appeared, what is BSC, how to use BSC, what the four-perspectives of BSC are and how the concept of indicators system in BSC works would be more clearly explained so that reader and especially managers should well understand. All these explanations would be used in chapter 4 to analyse how cause-and-effect correlations of implementing BSC in two German automobile industries so that the reader may evaluate whether BSC is a good strategic controlling instrument which may give benefits for these two German companies if BSC is applied.

Next, chapter 3 would present two examples of German automobile industries which had been implementing the concept of BSC in their companies and directly or indirectly stated that the concept of BSC had been properly applied in their strategy in achieving their objectives. Then, the facts shows BSC giving them more benefits in their company strategies would be shown with their financial reports for five years period so that it should clearly emphasis that this concept would deliver positive impacts especially for their financial reports.

In chapter 4, the analysis of using BSC is presented along with exploring out the cause-and-effect correlations from the result of implementing BSC in two German companies. Then, the analysis result of exploring out the advantages and disadvantages, which would probably happened, when this concept of BSC was applied or when BSC would be still applied in the future, would be carried out and shown. Furthermore, examining the chances and challenges of implementing BSC are two important themes since it shows the challenge for the managers if these are applied.

Finally, chapter 5 concludes and summarises this thesis

Chapter 2 BSC as A Strategic Controlling Instrument

2.1. Traditional Performance Measurement Concepts as Predecessor of BSC

According to Schmeisser, et al. (2011) the traditional concepts for the evaluation of corporate performance development are primarily focussed on monetary planning and controlling calculations which are able to express the company occurrences and gives effects on the company's profit. Furthermore, Schmeisser et al (2011) argued that the traditional performance measurement concepts (e.g., DuPont system, ZVEI-Ratio, Profit-Liquidity-ratio system) have a target to show the capacity and value flows within the company that deliver basic information for corporate management. They classified these concepts into three systems, as follows:

a) **DuPont system:**
   - The oldest and most well-known ratio system.
   - Developed by the American Chemical Corporation E.I. DuPont de Nemours and Company in 1919.
   - Illustrated as the pyramid which is Return on Investment (ROI) may be found on the top and may be the most important company goal because the key figure ROI is mathematically and practically broken down in its components in accordance with the annual report in statement of financial position and the profit and loss statement.

b) **ZVEI-ratio system:**
   - Developed by the Zentralverband der elektronischen Industrie (ZVEI) based on the DuPont ratio system in 1969.
   - Used as an analytical actual instrument and as a planning instrument for corporate management.
   - Involves the growth analysis (with four areas: sales activities, result, capital commitment, and value creation/occupation - with nine absolute indicators: sales, sales related result, period result, cash flow, inventories, fixed assets) and the structural analysis, which is the core of the ZVEI-ratio system, reviews the efficiency of a company.

- ➢ Consists of 210 indicators, of which 88 ratios are used most of the time. Most of the indicators are financial ratios, while non-financial ratios such as employee turnover or headcount are not often applied.
- ➢ Uses above all data from the financial statement, but does not fully renounce the use of indicators from cost and activity accounting.

c) **Profit-Liquidity-ratio system:**
- ➢ A multidimensional and operated more than the pure profit reasoning.
- ➢ Consist of a general part and a special part.
- ➢ The general part includes liquidity indicators such as CF, current surplus revenue, surplus scheduled and working capital) and a profit part (indicators: annual profit and deficit, ROA, ROI, rate of capital turnover, sales return, etc.)
- ➢ The special part involves indicators that are needed to complete the indicators of the general part which is appropriate with the individual company in dependence of the sector.

Furthermore, Schmeisser, et al. (2011) criticised that traditional Performance measurement concept using financial ratios, have many weaknesses since the historical data from accounting financial ratios only assess the current situation so that the future relevant actions and decisions of the management, e.g., innovations, quality and customer's satisfaction, may not be measured by financial ratios. In other words, traditional performance measurement systems may not be used to estimate long term success potentials of a company.

2.2. Comparing BSC with Traditional Performance Measurement

Based on Schmeisser, et al. (2011), traditional finance oriented for performance measurement instruments are not appropriate to the actual demands of the market because traditional finance oriented performance measurement instruments are only restricted to finance related targets so that they may be compared with modern, multidimensional, future oriented instruments for performance measurement which are not limited to measuring monetary targets only but also consider non-monetary, however, quantitative goals. The concept of BSC should be considered as multidimensional instrument which is described above.

In 2013, Lohrmann and Reichert stated to emphasise argument of Schmeisser, et al. (2011) after they compared BSC approach with traditional performance measurement concepts and stated that the concept of BSC recognises the financials as backwards-oriented and does not provide clarity on an organisation's future perspectives. Furthermore, organisational targets are often contradictory. For example, when its targets are maximising cash flow, it would be in contrast with the need for investment. Due to this reason the concept of BSC measures and controls organisational performance based on multiple perspectives. However, the concept of BSC does not only focus on one single perspective. It would try bringing the organisational goals to be addressed through its multiple dimensions. In other words, the organisational targets are combined into four perspectives (Financial, Customer, Innovation & Learning and Internal Business).

2.3. Controlling Instruments
2.3.1. Operational Instruments

Erichsen (2011, p. 9) defined operative instruments as a tool for an organisation to achieve its targets (e.g., profit and liquidity) based on short-term period (i.g., timeframe of one to two years) in order to ensure and to increase the profitability and efficiency of producing and selling its products. To achieve these targets, variety of controlling instruments is provided for management and managers (executives).

The critical point of the operational work of a controller (i.g., accountant) consists of planning; monitoring; controlling and the controller should be in cooperation and coordination with the executive employees of a company. Accordingly, instruments, such as operational planning, liquidity planning or calculation as well as instruments, such as discount analysis or project management, belong to tools which are used by operational controller. By these tools, management and managers may be regularly and promptly informed about the most important development which happens in company. He also characterises that operational controlling is always oriented with detailed figures, for example, turnovers in total, customer sales, product turnovers and cost data, for material and personnel or cost centre.

Then, we would be given the question, what actually the role of operational controlling are when it is confronted with strategic controlling which is only concerned with the question, how to efficiently and effectively exploit our new resources and provide additional resources?. Erichsen (2011, p. 9) argued that operational controlling is ideally arranging long-term targets and strategies then implementing them in daily business.

Erichsen (2011, pp. 9-195) named the following selection of operational controlling instruments may be used to help achieving the short-term targets, as follows: the ABC analysis, order-size analysis, reporting, break-even Analysis, product profitability calculation, bottleneck analysis, investment appraisal methods, liquidity planning, operational planning, project controlling, discount analysis, sales territory analysis and XYZ-Analysis.

2.3.2. Strategic instruments

Compared with operational controlling, strategic controlling applies different tools to lead a company to achieve its long-term targets. According to Erichsen (2011, p. 199), strategic controlling discusses about securing the existence of the company. It should be checked whether and where there are new potentials and opportunities for a company to achieve its targets.

In addition, he also stated that in topic of strategic controlling, it is necessary to recognise risk and how to prevent it. In other words, strategic controlling is considered for long-terms goals containing with risks and people working in controlling should be able to foresee effects which may happen and to prevent them so that it may give a positive impact for company and help managers to determine which strategies should be applied for company's success in attaining strategic targets and tasks.

Based on Erichsen (2011, p. 199), strategic targets and tasks of a company involve, as follows:

> ➢ **Product development:** for example, it should be considered to develop the product in order to be able to comply with dynamic customer expectation.
> ➢ **Development of new markets and customers:** for example, it may be tried to enter into global market after a company has successfully dominated local market so that it may give more challenges to recognise new customers with different request.
> ➢ **Improvement in productivity:** for example, in producing 200.000 cars per annum a company may discuss how to produce more than the initial plan with implementing the most sophisticated technologies in production.
> ➢ **Process improvement and organisational changes:** for example, to satisfy the customer request, companies need to review their production, sales, marketing process whether it has given benefits for customer or not.
> ➢ **Reduction in cost:** for example, reducing irrelevant costs may increase profit of company.
> ➢ **Risk analysis and prevention:** for example, as it has been described above.

Strategic controlling is reviewed for period of about one to five years in the future and is not commonly operated with detailed figures (e.g., turnovers or liquidity), but it provides analysis which is able to give informative, precise and explicit statement that may help managers in taking action for the further development of the company.

Although operational controlling and strategic controlling have different targets, they should be capable to work together and need to synchronise their targets in their daily work. For instance, when a company want to try entering new market with pointing the target of turnovers which increases 20% (for example, from 200 million Euro to 240 million Euro) in five years, a manager may inform its employees to observe the market first and especially to know what market wants and which products would be appropriate with that market. Then, the employees may implement that observation. For instance, they try producing and selling more than usual so that it may increase sales every year and achieve the target. In this part, operational controlling has tasks, for example, to plan which strategy should be applied, to control annually the turnovers whether has reached the target or not, to monitor its employees and company's development.

According to Erichsen (2011, pp. 199-389), instruments which may be used in strategic controlling to achieve the long-term goals of company and to deliver guidelines for daily operational business, are, as follows: Balanced Scorecard, Benchmarking, competitor analysis, Life-Cycle Costing, Portfolio-Analysis, potential analysis, risk controlling, strategic gap analysis, SWOT-Analysis and target costs management.

This bachelor thesis would only focus on the one strategic controlling instrument which is balanced scorecard. It would be completely explained and started from following chapter.

2.4. Balanced Scorecard (BSC)

Disselkamp & Schüller (2004) stated that in the early 1990s, the concept of balanced scorecard was developed by Robert S. Kaplan and David P. Norton who had closed cooperation with twelve American companies. Then, Lehr (2010) argued that the concept of balanced scorecard was introduced by Kaplan and Norton for the first time in 1992 in the journal of "Harvard Business Review".

Nowadays, BSC has been familiar for people who are working as a manager, a controller, and an accountant. This concept provides simplicity for managers through its concept which is multidimensional. Kaplan & Norton (1996, p. 2) argued that:

> "The Balanced Scorecard (BSC) provides managers with the instrumentation they need to navigate to future competitive success. Today, organizations are competing in complex environments so that an accurate understanding of their goals and the methods for attaining those goals is vital". Additionally, "The scorecard measures organizational performance across four balanced perspectives: financial, customers, internal business processes, and learning and growth. The BSC enables companies to track financial results while simultaneously monitoring progress in building the capabilities and acquiring the intangible assets they need for future growth".

Taguchi, Kaneko and Tabe (2009, p. 164) argued that balances in the BSC may be indicated into the balance between short-term and long-term objectives, the balance between the past, present and future, the balance between financial and non-financial perspectives, and the balance between internal and external perspectives. This argument stresses that BSC is a complete strategic controlling tool that should be implemented in a company and may be trusted to bring other perspectives for a company.

Figure 2 – Balanced Scorecard Illustrated as a Cockpit of an Airplane.
(Source: Nafatni, 2012)

Based on Kaplan & Norton (1996), the manager has role as a pilot, the company is represented as an airplane and the cockpit is assumed as a tool for manager which is BSC steering where the company would be brought and where to bring the company to reach the intended objectives. They assumed that in the cockpit, there are a lot of devices founded to navigate the airplane. Furthermore, through the cockpit the manager may navigate not only one factor (for example, wind) but also there are many factors (for instance, temperature, speed, etc.) which are also necessary to be monitored to bring the journey towards excellent future results. Kaplan & Norton's argument is added by Poureisa, Ahmadgourabi and Efteghar (2013) who agreed that this concept should be very helpful and appropriate for the top manager.

2.4.1. Implementation of BSC

According to Savkin (2011, p. 20), the company works usually with the strategy which is made by CEO or top-management. CEO makes a specific business strategy and then determines the particular targets to the lower level employees. The lower level managers convert the global strategic targets into specific business works that are necessary to be finished in order to achieve the strategic goal. In the end, these specific works are explained to the low level employee to be executed. In this part, the concept of BSC may be used as systematic approach which may translate the global target to the end-level employee. As a result, the idea of CEO may be easily understood on each level. From this point of view, it may be argued that BSC has an ability to explain the strategy to employees on each level and it is possible to be used to explain the strategy due to his opinion that BSC contains some indicators which would be connected to the company's main goals.

Furthermore, Weber and Schäffer (2008, p. 149) stated that the concept of balanced scorecard may be applied as a measurement system and then it may be used as a tool to connect company's strategy with its operations. In other words, when a manager has had a strategy for the company then the manager may insert BSC into its strategy in order to help a manager implement its strategy or take action. They also argued that this concept is reliable to connect between strategies with its operations.

The PEA in 1998 has also characterised the "Balanced Scorecard" approach as their chosen approach for deploying strategic direction, communicating expectations, and measuring progress towards agreed-to objectives.

According to PEA (1998, pp. 15-16), in the concept of BSC it is necessary to create vision, mission statement, and strategy for the company in order to ensure that the performance measures may be developed in each perspective to support in achieving the company's strategic targets and it also helps employees visualise and understand the connection between the performance measures and successful accomplishment of strategic targets.

Furthermore, PEA (1998, pp. 15-16) argued that it is necessary to identify what the company should do well (i.e., the performance objectives) in order to achieve the vision which has been targeted. For each objective, it is important to know the measures and to arrange goals relating to a reasonable period of time (for example, three to five years). It does not sound complex, however many variables have impact how long this exercise would take. For instance, how many employees that a company has and how many of them who are involved in setting the vision, mission, measures, and goals. BSC may be implemented to translate a company's vision into a set of performance objectives related in four perspectives of BSC: Financial, Customer, Internal Business Process, and Learning and Growth.

PEA (1998, pp. 15-16) explained that:

> "Some objectives are maintained to measure an organization's progress toward achieving its vision. Other objectives are maintained to measure the long term drivers of success. Through the use of the BSC, an organization monitors both its current performance (financial, customer satisfaction, and business process results) and its efforts to improve processes, motivate and educate employees, and enhance information systems - its ability to learn and improve."

Figure 3 below provides matrices applied in the concept of BSC. It may help managers to develop their objectives and measures. The matrices may be easily understood, but PEA (1998, pp. 15-16) argued that developing the contents of each matrix was not easy.

When creating performance measures, PEA (1998, pp. 15-16) recommended to ensure that performance measures should be connected to the strategic vision of the company and the measurement should concentrate on the results necessary to reach the company vision and the objectives of the strategic plan. Each objective within a perspective needs to be supported by at least one measurement indicating a company's performance against that objective. If a measure is executable and plausible, then its implementation should be supported.

PEA (1998, pp. 15-16) argued that:

> "When developing measures, it is important to include a mix of quantitative and qualitative measures. Quantitative measures provide more objectivity than qualitative measures. They may help to justify critical management decisions on resource allocation (e.g., budget and staffing) or systems improvement".

A manager should first identify any available quantitative data and review how it may support the objectives and measures incorporated in the BSC.

PEA (1998, pp. 15-16) defined qualitative measures as the matters of perception and it tends to be subjective. Furthermore, it is important to care with judgements based on the experience of customers, employees, managers and contractors since they provide important insights into acquisition performance and outcomes.

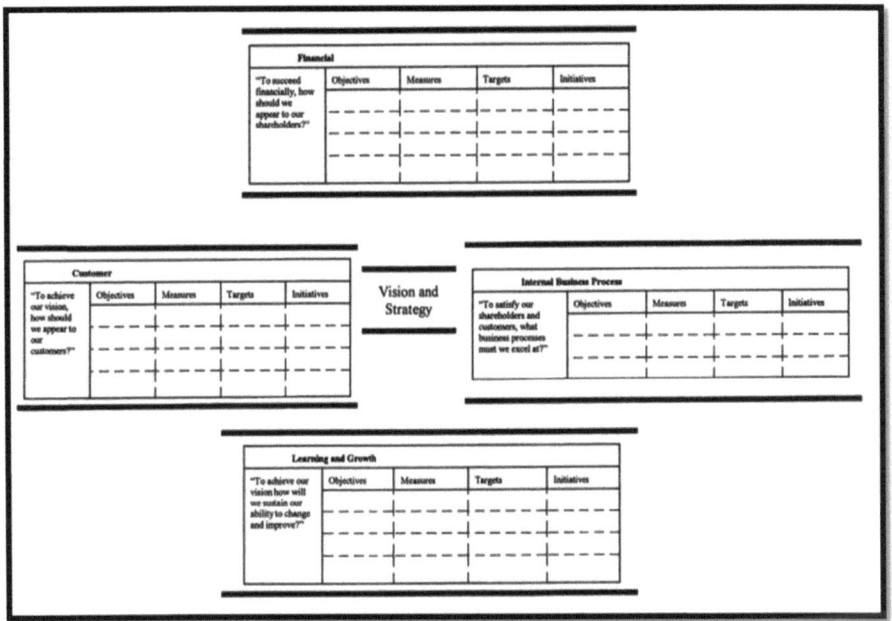

Figure 3 – Matrices Used in the BSC.
Source: Procurement Executives' Association (1998, p. 18)

In their website, help.sap.com (n.d.) stated that a completed BSC would become the focus of company alteration. People's goals, investments, and activities should all be connected to the objectives and the measurement of the scorecard. Because of that, it is important that this scorecard should be accurately designed to reflect the corporate strategy. According to help.sap.com (n.d.), a good Balanced Scorecard is designed with three principles that connect the measures to strategy:

1. **Cause-and-Effect Relationships:** A strategy containing with cause and effect. A properly designed scorecard may tell the story of the business unit's strategy through a series of cause-and-effect relationships. The measurement system should be explicitly related to objectives so that they may be arranged and validated. Every selected BSC's objective should become a part of a chain of cause-and-effect relationships that communicates about what the business unit's strategy means to the company.
2. **Outcomes and Performance Drivers:** All Balanced Scorecards apply some certain universal measures. These universal measures (i.e., market share, profitability, and customer satisfaction) are result-oriented measurement describing goals common across many strategies and industries. The performance indicators or the lead indicators are unique since they are used for a particular strategy. A good Balanced Scorecard consists of an appropriate mix of results (lagging indicators) and performance indicators (leading indicators) which have been adjusted to the business unit's strategy.

3. **Connection to Financials:** According to SAP (n.d.), it is not hard anymore to achieve our targets (quality, customer satisfaction, innovation, and the like) because of the proliferation of change programs under way in most companies today and a Balanced Scorecard should stay on results, especially financial ones. Finally, causal paths from all the measures on a scorecard should be connected to financial objectives.

SAP is a German multinational software company who developed a program related to the concept of Balanced Scorecard called SAP's Balanced Scorecard solution which is fully integrated into the SAP Strategic Enterprise Management (SEM) and fully supports these capabilities. It supports the development and maintenance process of a Balanced Scorecard.

After we have heard more about implementation of BSC above, Kaplan & Norton (1993) as the founding father of BSC concept impressed that the balanced scorecard is not a template that may be applied to businesses in general or industry-wide. Different market situations, product strategies, and competitive environments require different scorecards. Business units devise customised scorecards to fit their mission, strategy, technology, and culture.

2.4.2. Targets and tasks of BSC

Help.sap.com (n.d.) stated:
> "Using the Balanced Scorecard, corporate executives can now measure how their business units create value for current and future customers. They can also learn what investments in people, systems, and procedures are necessary to improve future performance. While retaining an interest in financial performance, the Balanced Scorecard clearly reveals the drivers of superior, long-term value and competitive performance. The Balanced Scorecard tells the story of the strategy".

"The scorecard should tell the story of the strategy, starting with the long-run financial objectives, and then linking them to the sequence of actions that must be taken with financial processes, customers, internal processes, and finally employees and systems to deliver the desired long-run economic performance." (Kaplan & Norton, 1996, p. 47)

In an article of Harvard Business Review written by Kaplan and Norton (1993), Larry D. Brady stated that the concept of balanced scorecard translates business unit strategies into a measurement system that connects with entire system of management.

Hirt (2015, pp. 251-252) argued that Balanced Scorecard as a very helpful instrument may forward a corporate vision to the operational actions. In other words, BSC enable each employee to indicate what employee should do to achieve corporate targets which are clearly constructed with the additional information of its indicators and then these targets are transformed to be a tangible action. Implementation of BSC in company is needed a certain openness and transparency in relation to all hierarchical levels in company. Furthermore, before starting implementation of BSC, it should be reviewed in order to make this instrument harmonised with its corporate culture. Recall what Kaplan and Norton (1998) has argued that implementation of balanced scorecard depends on its business, because different market situations, product strategies, and competitive environments require different scorecards.

Departed from explanations of each author above, it may be pulled a conclusion about targets and tasks of BSC are measuring of business units, telling story of strategy and connecting the long-term financial objectives to actions in order to help company in easily achieving its vision and its mission.

2.5. The four-perspectives of BSC

Figure 4 – Balanced Scorecard Strategic Perspectives
Source: Procurement Executives' Association (1998, p. 8)

According to Sherwood, Clark and Lynas (2005, p. 83), the four perspectives of BSC are started from "The trust of Kaplan and Norton's thesis that traditional financial measures such as return on investment or earnings per share are good only for reporting results and that these metrics are not very useful in helping to make the effective strategic decisions that lead to the results", so that it enables to launch other three perspectives as seen above in figure 4.

Mooraj, Oyon and Hostettler (1999, p. 482) stated that the original BSC is designed to identify four perspectives which are the financial perspective, the customer perspective, the internal-business-process perspective, and the learning and growth perspective so that its perspectives represent three of the main stakeholders of the business (i.g., shareholders, customers and employees), thereby, they are ensuring that an entire view of the company is applied for strategic reflection and implementation. However, it is important to know that the chosen perspectives (no matter how many are chosen to be necessary) and the measure are consistent with the corporate strategy.

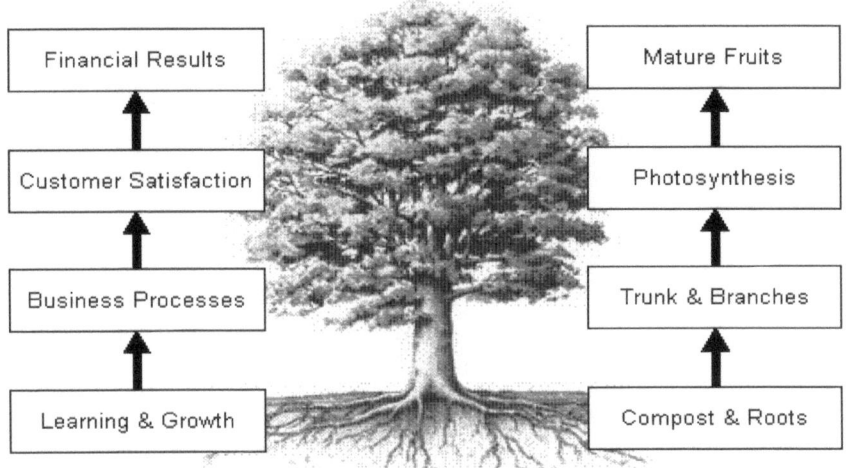

Figure 5 – The Four Perspectives of BSC Illustrated as a Process of Planting an Apple Tree.
Source: http://www.business-process-it.com/balanced-scorecard.html (2008).

From the figure 5, the four perspectives of BSC may be explained in a process of planting an apple tree when a manager which may be illustrated as a gardener tries planting an apple tree. His final target that he wants to achieve is obtaining the best fruits from his apple tree and this target represents a financial perspective or financial results. To achieve his target, it would be needed to take care of his apple tree. Starting from providing the best quality of compost, feeding them with fertilisers and water which are these fundamental processes described as providing training programmes that support business process illustrated as trunk and branches which are continuously growing and followed by arising of leaves. The growth of this apple tree is then followed with emergence of apple fruits through processes of photosynthesis which may represent a customer satisfaction.

Because of that the necessary connections through all four scorecard perspectives are needed to settle the financial themes of increasing revenues, improving cost and productivity, enhancing asset utilisation, and reducing risk (Kaplan & Norton, 1996, p. 47).

2.5.1. Financial

According to Mooraj, Oyon and Hostettler (1999, p. 482), the financial perspective reflects the long-term objectives of the company. The chosen measures would represent the relevant level in the product or service life-cycle and are outlined by Kaplan and Norton in 1996 as rapid growth, sustain and harvest.

> ➢ Financial objectives for the growth level would be mostly represented by sales volumes, existing and new customer relationships and process development.
> ➢ The sustain level would be based on measures analysing ROI, for instance: ROCE, discounted cash flow and EVA.
> ➢ The harvest level would be represented by analysing cash flow with measures (e.g., payback periods and revenue volume).

Schmeisser, et al. (2011, pp. 35-36) added the Balanced Scorecard as a multi-target-oriented method integrating the value of the management through the financial perspective. Moreover, in financial perspective, a company usually tends to discuss how to fulfil the financial expectations of the shareholders and it would be poured into company targets. Because of that, it is necessary to fulfil the goals of the shareholders such as profit and growth purposes and all strategies, programs and initiatives are focused towards the achievement of the long-term company purpose, the generation of financial profits for the investors. Furthermore, the financial perspective is defined as final objective and it is connected to the customer, internal process and learning and development perspective through cause-and-effect relations.

2.5.2. Customer

Then, Mooraj, Oyon and Hostettler (1999, p. 482) defined that the customer perspective is composed of measures relating to the most desired (i.e., the most profitable) customer groups. These measures involve some standard measures, for example, customer satisfaction and customer retention and they should be adjusted in order to be appropriate with the company requirements.

According to Schmeisser, et al. (2011, pp. 36-37), the customer perspectives consist of strategic purposes of a company which are linked to the customers and market segments, on which it wants to compete. These strategic purposes should be the customers and market oriented so that the satisfaction of customers are defined as the achievement. However, these customers satisfaction should be followed together with financial goals. Since the customers who are buyers of the products have influence in up and down value of the earnings of a company, it is needed to identify characteristics of company which positively influences on the purchase decision. It is necessary to use these indicators such as the market share or the customer loyalty and it is also important to identify the product and service characteristics as well as the customer relations.

2.5.3. Internal business process

The internal-business process perspective emphasises on the internal processes which are able to be expected by customers regarding the value of productivity and efficiency may be improved (Mooraj, Oyon and Hostettler, 1999, pp. 482-483).

Schmeisser, et al. (2011, p. 37) argued that the perspectives processes and learning and development reflect the resource-oriented method of strategic management which is described as solving customer problems and achieving competitive advantages through a specific combination of available and developing resources. In other words, to fulfil customer wishes, it is also important to identify our internal processes because it is connected with the targets of the financial and customer perspective. For example, to reach high customer loyalty, it is needed the customers' value requirements which has been complied and from that, it would logically lead an increase in financial profits and then, the shareholders are automatically satisfied and they (2011, p. 37) also appended that it is necessary to have competitive internal system and performance processes to satisfy the customers. For that, Kaplan and Norton (1996, p. 27) have also stated that the internal-business-process indicators emphasise on the internal processes that lead the greatest impact on customer satisfaction and achieving an company's financial objectives.

According to Kaplan and Norton (1996, p. 27) the value chain of internal business process consists of:

- **Innovation process:** the fulfilment of new request of current or future customers may be started with designing and developing of new product.
- **Operation process:** it is considerate how to manufacture and market this new product and how about its cost and quality.
- **The customer service process**: it is considered how to increase the customer satisfaction and it is more discussing about services for customers.

2.5.4. Learning and growth

The learning and growth perspective stress on internal skills and capabilities, in order to adjust them to the strategic goals of the company. The Balanced Scorecard is processed to analyse spaces between the required and existing skills and capabilities. BSC may be used to determine what strategic initiatives and related measures should be taken to close the spaces so that these spaces may then be addressed and closed by initiatives such as staff training and development (Mooraj, Oyon and Hostettler, 1999, p. 483).

By looking at learning and growth perspective, Kaplan and Norton (1996, p. 28) expected that the company creates long-term growth and improvement because it is impossible to match the long-term targets for customers and internal processes with just applying today's technologies and capabilities. They also argued that in intense global competition it is necessary for companies to continually improve their capabilities for delivering value to customers and shareholders.

Kaplan and Norton (1996, pp. 28) argued that:

> "Organizational learning and growth come from three principal sources: people, systems, and organizational procedures. The financial, customer, and internal-business-process objectives on the Balanced Scorecard typically will reveal large gaps between the existing capabilities of people, systems, and procedures and what will be required to achieve breakthrough performance".

Nevertheless, these gaps may be closed through providing additional coaching/training for employees, investing in upgrading information technology and systems and investing in aligning corporate procedures and routines (Kaplan and Norton, 1996, pp. 28-29).

2.6. Strategic targets formulated in the four perspectives

Erichsen (2011, p. 208) presented an example of formulating strategic targets into four perspectives, as follows:

a. Financial perspective:
- Increasing annual revenue faster and bigger than the market.
- Doubling cash flow within three years.
- Achieving market leadership within five years.
- Increasing productivity per account by 80% compared to previous years.
- Arousing cost awareness among all employees.
- Generating Return on equity of at least 15%.

b. **Customer perspective:**
- Increasing the number of regular customers within three years to 50%.
- Improving customer profitability by 50%.
- Increasing customer satisfaction by 15% annually.
- Acquiring new customers.
- Increasing customer loyalty.
- Increasing market share by 5-8% per year.

c. **Internal Business Process perspective:**
- Improving preparation times within three years by at least 50%.
- Reducing periods of time of development and Innovation by 50%.
- Achieving Quality Improvement.
- Reducing processing times in the production by 15%.
- Making loan decision process by 50% faster.
- Reducing delivery times and transmission routes.

d. **Learning and Growth Perspective:**
- Improving staff qualifications.
- Achieving continuous improvement.
- Increasing employee satisfaction.
- Reducing staff turnover by 10%.
- Implementing of EFQM.
- Increasing number of new products on sales.

2.7. The concept of indicators system

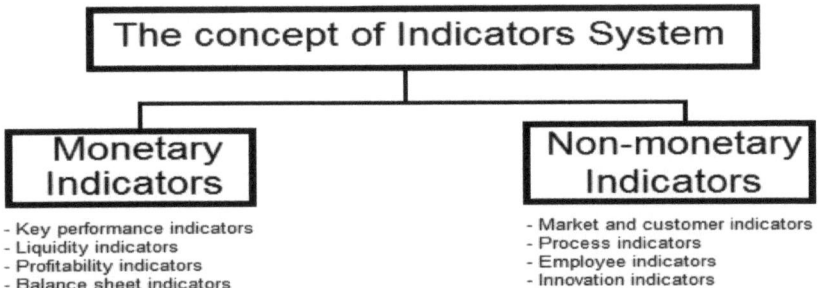

Figure 6 – The Concept of Indicators System.
Source: haufe.de (n.d.)

Through balanced scorecard as strategic management system, the corporate strategies are operationalised and made measureable with the aid of strategic goals, indicators, annual targets and actions, as argued by Schmeisser & Claussen (2009). An Indicator is needed in the concept of balanced scorecard, because through indicators a manager may measure the performance of company, for example, knowing whether the company has achieved its targets or measuring how high the customer satisfaction is.

Erichsen (2011, p. 53) argued that indicators should transparently clearly represent the complex facts and circumstances. Furthermore, a single parameter mostly is constructed from different figures. Because of that, it enables each indicator may explain how the situation of company so that a decision maker should be helped to take the right decision.

In the study of PEA in 1998, PEA stated that the concept of BSC is used to translate a corporate strategic objective into a set of performance into a set of performance indicators which is inserted among four perspectives. PEA argued that some indicators are applied to measure a corporate progress toward attaining its vision and other indicators are applied to know the long-term drivers of success.

Based on von der Gathen (2014, p. 180), the term of "Balanced" refers to the "not less" and "not more" between short-term and long-term objectives, monetary and non-monetary indicators as well (e.g., shareholder and customer-related) between external and internal (e.g., processes and employee-related) measures. Moreover, he (2014, p. 180) stated that the "Balanced" is also based on looking at the whole company, for example, financial as well as non-financial performance indicators should be used.

Jahnke & Sassmann's (2003, p. 344) came up and stated that the BSC combines objects and basic information relating to the principles of cause-and-effect and compilation of performance indicators (e.g., early-indicators, influence factors, performance-indicators, value-indicators such as lead-time, failure time) and result key-data (e.g., late-indicators such as profitability, market share, customer satisfaction, customer loyalty, employees' qualification) and it is similar as stated by Gabriel (2004) that the Balanced Scorecard Method emphasises the observation of early and late indicators. For example, when a company has made a target to increase its customer satisfaction, the company may struggle how to reduce the error rate as much as possible so that in the future, as a result, many customers are purchasing the good quality products and it would cause an increase of customer's satisfaction. In this part, early indicators may be indicated as an error rate which a company tries to reduce it and late indicators may be described as whether the company has successfully achieved its target with looking at its late indicators such as profitability, market share, customer satisfaction, customer loyalty, and employees' qualification.

Discussing about the relationship between monetary and non-monetary indicators in the concept of BSC, non monetary indicators have tasks to complete the monetary indicators which are able to be defined as financial indicators. Furthermore, monetary indicators are appropriate to monitor certain targets.

By giving a limited number of indicators which concentrate on key business processes by level of management, it enables to minimise information in implementing of BSC. For instance, both monetary and non-monetary indicators are frequently needed for lower levels of management, while top management needs summary and comprehensive monetary indicators (Grove, Cook and Richter, 2008, p. 3).

Grove, Cook and Richter (2008, p. 3) stated that commonly, non-monetary indicators are notified more often than monetary indicators. For instance, non-monetary, operating indicators, such as machine downtime, percentage of capacity used, and deviations from schedule, are probably measured every day. Other non-monetary indicators, such as manufacturing cycle time, delivery accuracy, customer complaints, and spoilage, are probably measured once a week. Some non-monetary and monetary indicators, such as inventory days, accounts receivable days, product returns, and warranty costs, are probably measured every three months. Other non-monetary and monetary indicators, such as new products introduced, market share, total cost of poor quality, return on investment and employee training are probably measured per year.

2.7.1. Monetary indicators

According to haufe.de (n.d.), target-oriented indicators consist of monetary and non-monetary indicators. The monetary indicators are composed of, as follows:
- Key performance indicators (e.g., Profit, EBIT, EBITDA, etc.),
- Liquidity indicators (e.g., Liquidity 1st to 3rd grade, cash flow, working capital, etc.),
- Profitability indicators (e.g., return on sales, return on equity, return on assets, return on capital employed (e.g., ROCE), return on investment (e.g., ROI), etc.) and
- Balance sheet indicators (e.g., equity ratio, debt ratio, leverage ratio, intensity of investment, etc.).

Thereof, monetary indicators are able to be linked to the financial perspective in concept of BSC.

2.7.2. Non-monetary indicators

Based on haufe.de (n.d.), non-monetary indicators involve, as follows:
- Market and customer indicators (e.g., market share, customer acquisition rate, etc.),
- Process indicators (e.g., error rate, capacity utilisation, level of service, etc.),
- Employee indicators (e.g., sickness absence rate, staff turnover rate, employee productivity, etc.) and
- Innovation indicators (e.g., innovation rate, research intensity, proposal rate, etc.).

Non-monetary indicators are more appropriate for customer-, Internal Business Process- and Learning & Growth Perspective. All of these non-monetary indicators are supporting monetary indicators to achieve its targets.

Chapter 3 Implementation of BSC in automobile industries

According to balancedscorecard.org, there are three German Companies listed who are implementing the concept of Balanced Scorecard. Two of them are automobile industries which are DaimlerChrysler and BMW Financial Services. I would analyse how the BSC has played a role within their strategies, whether both companies directly or indirectly observed concept of BSC in their strategies, and there are positive alterations to their financial reports if they inserted the concept of BSC. Through chapter 3.1 BSC at Daimler AG and chapter 3.2 BSC at BMW Group would be provided statements about the concept of BSC. Moreover, both chapters are also providing data from their annual reports in period of five years which may be used to show that with looking at and implementing this concept, it would cause positive impact for their monetary aspects such as revenue and EBIT.

3.1. BSC at Daimler AG

Based on their Daimler website (daimler.com), it is explained that Daimler AG, which was also named Daimlerchrysler from 1995 to 2007, is one of the world's most successful automotive companies and one of the biggest producers of premium cars and the world's biggest manufacturer of commercial vehicles with a global reach. Daimler AG involves five divisions such as Mercedes-Benz Cars, Daimler Trucks, Mercedes-Benz Vans, Daimler Buses and Daimler Financial Services. Besides manufacturing premium cars and commercial vehicles, Daimler AG in the division of Daimler Financial Services is providing financing, leasing, fleet management, insurance, financial investments, credit cards, and innovative mobility services. In Europe, North and South America, Asia, and Africa, Daimler AG has production facilities and sells its vehicles and services in nearly all the countries of the world. Furthermore, each division manages some products as seen below in figure 7, where Mercedes-Benz Cars Division manages its product portfolio such as Mercedes-Benz, Mercedes-AMG, Mercedes-Maybach, the brands Smart and Mercedes-Me which is currently appeared in 2015 according to this source: https://www.daimler.com/brands-and-products/our-brands. Then, Daimler Trucks division arranges its product portfolio such as Mercedes Benz; Freightliner; Western star; Thomas built buses; Fuso and Bharat-Benz. Mercedes-Benz Vanz division focuses on its product portfolio such as Mercedes-Benz Vanz and Freightliner. Daimler Buses is concentrated on its product such as Setra and Mercedes-Benz Bus. Finally, Daimler Financial Services division manages its product portfolio such as Mercedes-Benz Bank, Mercedes-Benz Financial Services, Daimler Truck Financial, Moovel and Car2Go.

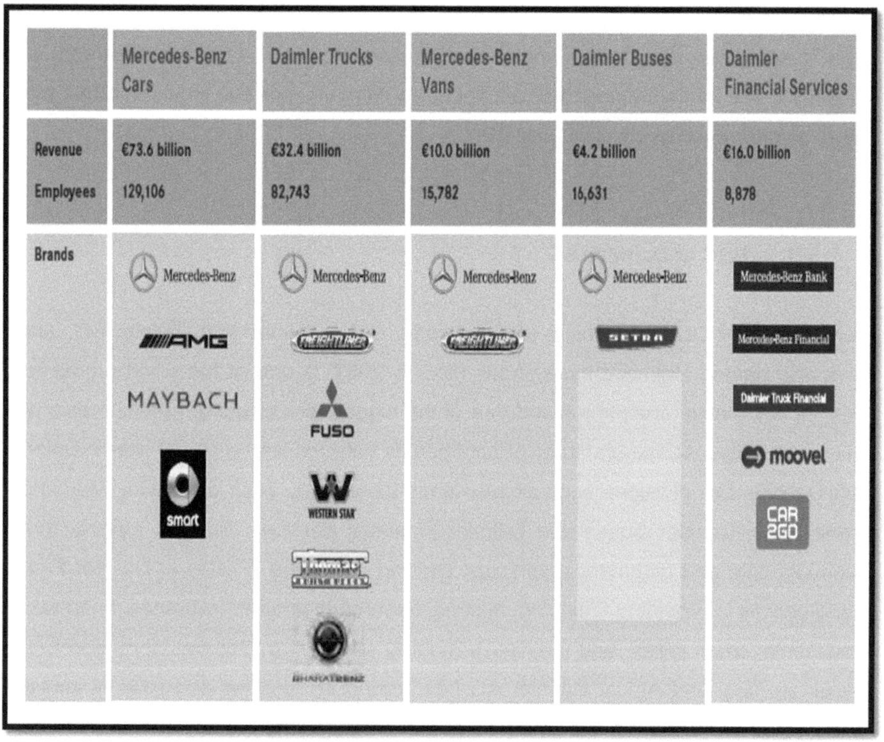

	Mercedes-Benz Cars	Daimler Trucks	Mercedes-Benz Vans	Daimler Buses	Daimler Financial Services
Revenue	€73.6 billion	€32.4 billion	€10.0 billion	€4.2 billion	€16.0 billion
Employees	129,106	82,743	15,782	16,631	8,878
Brands	Mercedes-Benz, AMG, MAYBACH, smart	Mercedes-Benz, FREIGHTLINER, FUSO, WESTERN STAR, THOMAS, BHARATBENZ	Mercedes-Benz, FREIGHTLINER	Mercedes-Benz, SETRA	Mercedes-Benz Bank, Mercedes-Benz Financial, Daimler Truck Financial, moovel, CAR2GO

Figure 7 – Product Portfolio of Daimler AG.
Source: Daimler's annual financial report (2014, p. 73)

On the stock exchanges of Frankfurt and Stuttgart, Daimler is listed with symbol of DAI. In 2014, more than 2.5 million vehicles were sold, 279,972 people were employed and Daimler AG increased its revenue by 10% to €129.9 billion. Furthermore, Daimler achieved EBIT of €10.8 billion in 2014.

Figure 8 – The Board of Management of Daimler AG.
Source: Daimler.com (2015)

Daimler's Board of Management now is chaired by Dr. Dieter Zetsche, who in 2004 stated that "The Balanced Scorecard provided the organisation with a clear roadmap of where we needed to go, as well as the methodology to measure our progress in reaching the aggressive targets we've set," (prnewswire.com, 2004, para. 3).

As stated above, that Zetsche has a positive argument about the concept of Balanced Scorecard. Since BSC focus not only on financial targets but also non-financial targets and since 2012, as already stated in financial report of Daimler AG (2014, p. 119), Daimler AG used non-financial targets as a basis for assessment, for example, to measure employee satisfaction, diversity, customer satisfaction or product quality, and the further development and permanent establishment of the corporate value of integrity.

However, starting from Zetsche's statement, how the implementation of BSC in Daimler AG would be seen from this part and how the concept of BSC affects to the monetary indicators which are showed through financial reports of Daimler AG within a period of five years (2010-2014).

In Daimler's annual financial reports (2014, p. 64), Daimler AG stated that:

> "As the inventor of the automobile, we believe it is our mission and our duty to shape future mobility in a safe and sustainable manner with outstanding products and services and trend-setting technologies. We strive to attain the leading position in all of our business. Our goals are to be the leader in technology and innovation, to inspire our customers, and to continue to grow profitably with first-class teams. In this way, we intend to continually increase our enterprise value."

Furthermore, as written in Daimler's annual financial report (2014, p. 64), Daimler also concentrates on four objectives, as follows:

- **Technology leadership and innovation:** Daimler applies standards for its technology and innovation in order to make its products from all divisions to be the industry leaders (e.g., safety, autonomous driving with cars and commercial vehicles, and green technologies.).
- **Delighted customers:** Daimler was targeting to be at the top of all relevant customer-satisfaction rankings and to be able to convince its customers with its outstanding quality (e.g., creating interface for sales and after-sales process)
- **Best teams:** Daimler works in teams whose diversity in terms of gender, nationality and age, so that it would be a credit to work at Daimler. Moreover, passion, respect, integrity and discipline are focussed as its core corporate values.

- **Profitable growth:** Daimler was targeting to achieve a return on sales of 9% (EBIT in relation to revenue) on average for the automotive business.

From a declaration of Daimler's statement and its four objectives above, the concept of BSC had been inserted and should be seen if we observe its statement and objectives. For example:

- **Financial perspective:** achieving a return on sales of 9% on average for the automotive business or increasing profits may be related to Daimler's financial target and its financial target represents its financial perspective.
- **Customer perspective:** to achieve its financial target above, Daimler AG tried to focus on customer satisfaction rankings. For example, improving services (e.g., sales and after sales) and shaping future mobility in a safe and sustainable manner with outstanding products and services and trend-setting technologies would automatically increase the customer satisfaction. In page 158 of Daimler AG's financial report (2014), Daimler AG also provides a program called "Best Customer Experience" which is established to ensure completely personalised service for customers (i.g., the initial contact to advice, test drives, purchases and after sales services).
- **Internal Business Process perspective:** having goal to be the leader in technology and innovation and implementing standards for its technology and innovation would deliver to invest more in development of its current technology and innovation. As a result, customers may be satisfied because they may obtain a high-quality and more sophisticated products.

> **Learning and Growth Perspective:** this perspective is related to employee satisfaction. For that, mostly Daimler's employees are proud to work there. Daimler AG provides a very good atmosphere for employees and Daimler AG hired employees without comparing at their gender, nationality and age. Furthermore, Daimler AG continuously provides training programs for employees and managers, as already written in Daimler Sustainability Report (2014, p. 46), training programs for employees and managers are continuously optimised and expended. Moreover, with the principle of lifelong learning, Daimler's employees obtain further education and training and Daimler also stated in Daimler Sustainability Report (2014, p. 63) that "Continuing education is regulated by the general works agreement on qualification, which also provides that employees can leave the company for up to five years in order to obtain additional qualifications, and can subsequently return to the company."

As already written in Daimler Sustainability Report (2014, p. 75), the financial performance indicators used at Daimler AG have orientation towards investors' interests and wishes. To measure operating profit at divisional level, Daimler AG uses EBIT which is calculated before interest and income taxes and it can represent the divisions' profit and loss responsibility.

According to Daimler Sustainability Report (2014, p. 76), apart from EBIT and revenue, the important financial indicators for measuring Daimler's operating financial performance involve the free cash flow of the industrial business, investment, and research and development expenditure. However, not only looking at financial indicators but Daimler AG also pays attention to various non-financial indicators to help them arrange the Group. In addition, according to the context of Daimler's sustainability management, non-financial indicators are applied to measure CO_2 emissions of its vehicle fleet and to measure how much energy and water are consumed in its production sites. Furthermore, Daimler AG uses non-financial indicators to take decision of the compensation for Daimler's Board of Management members.

Implementing the concept of BSC at Daimler AG was already reported in Daimler Sustainability Report (2011, p. 101), where "Commitment to Excellence" become as philosophy of Daimler procurement business which is defined by the Daimler Supplier Network (DSN). This philosophy is related to the principles of performance and partnership. The External Balanced Scorecard was introduced to help Daimler AG in measuring its suppliers' performance according to the criteria of quality, technology, costs, and delivery reliability. The principle of partnership involves the aspects of fairness, reliability, and credibility. Moreover, as already defined in Daimler's Jahresfinanzbericht (2009, p. 254), the External Balanced Scorecard is an instrument used to development of strategic suppliers. In order words, as stated in DaimlerChrysler Annual Report (2001, p. 49) that DaimlerChrysler used this External Balanced Scorecard approach to measure the suppliers potential in terms of quality, system costs, technology and delivery effectiveness in a structured manner. These measurements should be reviewed and applied to develop new methods to improve weak sites. This External Balanced Scorecard is not only able to be an important Instrument for increasing performance but also help the joint goal-agreement process.

Furthermore, Sustainability strategy, which is applied at Daimler AG, leads Daimler AG to reach its long-term success in harmony with the environment and society. As written In page 101 of Daimler AG's financial report (2014),

> "Our sustainability strategy has six core aspects ("dimensions of responsibility"), to which relevant areas have been assigned where action needs to be taken. We have linked them with targets and target indicators. Together, all of our goals and targets serve as the basis for our medium- to long-term Sustainability Program 2020, which we use to measure our performance, although we also wish our performance to be judged externally. Sustainability Program 2020 also defines the areas in which we plan to take action in the coming years. For example, we aim to further reduce pollutants and emissions, further enhance the safety of our vehicles, and further expand and more systematically structure our efforts to protect human rights."

The result of this sustainability strategy should be seen in its products which are very safe driven. For example, ADAC (n.d.) announced that Mercedes C-class, which is a premium style sedan manufactured from 2014, has passed a crash test directed by

German auto association ADAC and scored five stars of overall evaluation which consists of occupant protection (92%), child safety (84%), pedestrian safety (77%) and safety equipment (70%). Compared to China's Brilliance BS6 (Model 2007 to 2010) which is also positioned as a premium style import sedan at a budget price and developed for the European market, failed in ADAC's crash test and only scored one star of overall evaluation as written in Autobild.de (2007) and announced by uk.reuters.com (2007). Tham (2013) argued that Chinese car companies lag on research and development. Furthermore, Tham (2013) inserted statement of Nat Ahrens, Deputy Director and Fellow of the Hills Program on Governance at CSIS, that most Chinese companies are considering five to six years out with their research and development spending compared to the international companies which are already considering twenty to twenty five years out.

Figure 9 – ADAC Crash-test Brilliance BS6.
Source: Autobild.de in: http://www.autobild.de/artikel/adac-crashtest-brilliance-bs6-220767.html (2007)

Figure 10 – ADAC's Crash-test for Mercedes C-class.
Source: ADAC in: https://www.adac.de/infotestrat/tests/crash-test/detail.aspx?IDtest=447

Next, we look at financial aspect and table 1 below would show the five years summary of Daimler AG's financial report from the statements of income and it is related to financial perspective of BSC. From table 1 should be seen positive revenue and EBIT which belong to key performance indicators.

According to table 1, from 2010 to 2014 Daimler AG's revenue and EBIT show positive movement meaning good sign for the company.

	2010	2011	2012	2013	2014
Amounts in millions of euros					
From the statements of income					
Revenue	97,761	106,540	114,297	117,982	129,872
Personnel expenses [1, 2]	16,454	17,424	18,002	18,753	19,607
Research and development expenditure [3]	4,849	5,634	5,644	5,489	5,680
thereof capitalized	1,373	1,460	1,465	1,284	1,148
Operating profit/EBIT [2]	7,274	8,755	8,820	10,815	10,752
Operating margin (%) [2]	7.4	8.2	7.7	9.2	8.3
Income/Profit (loss) before income taxes and extraordinary items [2]	6,628	8,449	8,116	10,139	10,173
Net operating income/ Net operating profit (loss) [2]	5,120	6,240	7,302	9,173	7,678
as % of net assets (RONA) [2]	17.5	19.9	19.6	22.6	18.8
Net income/Net profit (loss) [2]	4,674	6,029	6,830	8,720	7,290
Net income per share (€)/ Net profit (loss) per share (€) [2]	4.28	5.32	6.02	6.40	6.51
Diluted net income per share (€)/ Diluted net profit (loss) per share (€) [2]	4.28	5.31	6.02	6.40	6.51
Total dividend	1,971	2,346	2,349	2,407	2,621
Dividend per share (€)	1.85	2.20	2.20	2.25	2.45

[1] Until August 3, 2007, including Chrysler.

[2] For the year 2012, the figures have been adjusted, primarily for effects arising from application of the amended version of IAS 19.

[3] The figure for 2013 has been adjusted due to reclassifications within functional costs.

Table 1 – Five Years Summary of Daimler AG's Financial Report 2014.
Source: Daimler's annual financial report (2014, p. 286)

3.2. BSC at BMW Group

„Bayerische Motoren Werke Aktiengesellschaft (BMW AG), which is based in Munich, Germany, is the parent company of the BMW Group", stated in annual report of BMW Group (2014, p. 18). According to bmwgroup.com, The BMW Group manufactures not only automobiles but also motorcycles worldwide. The vehicles are manufactured with the highest standards in terms of aesthetics, dynamics, technology and quality. Moreover, the BMW Group also has a similarity compared to Daimler AG offering financial services. Nevertheless, the difference with Daimler AG is located on manufacturing motorcycles. Daimler AG does not manufacture motorcycle, while BMW Group does with the BMW brand. BMW Group entirely focuses on premium standards and outstanding quality for all its brands and across all relevant segments. BMW, MINI as well as Rolls-Royce are three of the strongest premium brands in the automobile industry.

Discussing about its strategy, BMW website (bmwgroup.com) explains that the BMW Group has applied "Strategy Number ONE" and this strategy is aligned with two targets which are "to be profitable and to enhance long-term value in times of change". Then, this strategy is applied to technological, structural and cultural aspects of BMW's company. Moreover, since 2007, BMW Group's strategy is based on four pillars: "Growth, Shaping the Future, Profitability and Access to Technologies and Customers". In its website, BMW Group also stated its mission which would be valid up to the year 2020 that the BMW Group should be the world's leader in providing premium products and premium services for individual mobility. Therefore it should be seen that BMW AG has the same thought compared with Daimler AG that considers long-term period. Sustainability is valued as an important factor for their company's growth.

Figure 11 – Corporate Facts: Board of Management of BMW Group.
Source: Bmwgroup.com (2015)

Based on BMW's website, the board of management of BMW AG chaired by Harald Krüger since May 13th in 2015, determined "sustainability" as a key corporate principle back in 2000. "The main goal was to integrate sustainability throughout the entire value chain and its underlying processes - creating an added value for the company, the environment and society", written in its website related to the topic of Sustainability Strategy - Turning vision into reality. Moreover, according to bmwgroup.com (2008, p. 9), "sustainability" was determined Group-wide as a corporate target. The definition of balanced scorecard is explained on BMW Group's Glossary and BSC has some tasks to document and measure the results of a company's activities against its vision and strategies. Furthermore, BSC may provide managers a comprehensive overview of the performance and efficiency of their organisation. BSC considers not only human factors in results but also financial aspects. Therefore, detailed guidelines have been developed for all BMW Group divisions (e.g., Finance, Production, Development, Motorcycles Production, Purchasing and Supplier Network, Human Resources, etc.).

According to Bauer (2010, pp. 433-443), who had been CEO of BMW Group Financial Services, BMW Group Financial Services decided to use the concept of Balanced Scorecard for integration of strategy formulation (e.g., competitive and environmental analyses, SWOT-Analysis), strategy implementation (e.g., operationalising the strategy, behaviour control, Organisational Alignment) and strategic learning (e.g., best-practice Sharing, monitoring of implementation) in a consistent management process. Bauer (2010, pp. 433-443) also stated that after this concept was introduced, BMW Group Financial Services identified ten key success factors of implementing BSC, as follows:

1. The BSC-Introduction should be defined as strategic Change-Project, not as a pure Performance-Measurement-Project which only delivers the additional indicators and reports.
2. For Introducing BSC, managements from all levels and divisions of organisation should be intensive involved.
3. The BSC-Introduction is not an IT-issue, but it initially extends to Standard Office Software. In other words, IT-Tool may be used to support this concept.

4. Top Management should promptly and transparent communicate the vision, mission, strategy map and BSC to all employees.
5. The BSC should be well understood by each employee so that employees understand what they should do and they should clearly recognise what objectives they should achieve.
6. The BSC should be the main document to determine company objective for all management levels.
7. The allocation of budgets and all other resources should be clearly based on the outlined Strategy Map.
8. The concept of BSC should be active used in all management meetings.
9. The cross-functional team work has to be supported by top management.
10. The BSC should be clear and transparent connected to the performance appraisal system to remind employees about their accountability.

Hereafter, it would be provided table 2 which displays non-financial performance indicators related to the concept of balanced scorecard. Non-financial indicators or non-monetary indicators may show indicators which should answer the questions such as how much vehicles have successfully been manufactured and sold by BMW Group for five years period.

BMW Group in figures

	2010	2011	2012	2013	**2014**	Change in %
Principal non-financial performance indicators						
BMW Group						
Workforce at end of year[1]	95,453	100,306	105,876	110,351	**116,324**	5.4
Automotive segment						
Sales volume[2]	1,461,166	1,668,982	1,845,186	1,963,798	**2,117,965**	7.9
Fleet emissions in g CO_2/km[3]	148	145	143	133	**130**	–2.3
Motorcycles segment						
Sales volume[4]	98,047	104,286	106,358	115,215	**123,495**	7.2
Further non-financial key performance figures						
Automotive segment						
Sales volume						
BMW[2]	1,224,280	1,380,384	1,540,085	1,655,138	**1,811,719**	9.5
MINI	234,175	285,060	301,526	305,030	**302,183**	–0.9
Rolls-Royce	2,711	3,538	3,575	3,630	**4,063**	11.9
Total[2]	<u>1,461,166</u>	<u>1,668,982</u>	<u>1,845,186</u>	<u>1,963,798</u>	<u>2,117,965</u>	<u>7.9</u>
Production volume						
BMW[5]	1,236,989	1,440,315	1,547,057	1,699,835	**1,838,268**	8.1
MINI	241,043	294,120	311,490	303,177	**322,803**	6.5
Rolls-Royce	3,221	3,725	3,279	3,354	**4,495**	34.0
Total[5]	<u>1,481,253</u>	<u>1,738,160</u>	<u>1,861,826</u>	<u>2,006,366</u>	<u>2,165,566</u>	<u>7.9</u>
Motorcycles segment						
Production volume[6]						
BMW	99,236	110,360	113,811	110,127	**133,615**	21.3
Financial Services segment						
New contracts with retail customers	1,083,154	1,196,610	1,341,296	1,471,385	**1,509,113**	2.6

[1] Figures exclude suspended contracts of employment, employees in the non-work phases of pre-retirement part-time arrangements and low income earners.
[2] Including the joint venture BMW Brilliance Automotive Ltd., Shenyang (2010: 53,701 units, 2011: 94,400 units, 2012: 141,165 units, 2013: 198,542 units, 2014: 275,891 units).
[3] EU-28.
[4] Excluding Husqvarna, sales volume up to 2013: 59,776 units.
[5] Including the joint venture BMW Brilliance Automotive Ltd., Shenyang (2010: 55,588 units, 2011: 98,241 units, 2012: 150,052 units, 2013: 214,920 units, 2014: 287,466 units).
[6] Excluding Husqvarna, production up to 2013: 59,426 units.

Table 2 – Five Years Summary of Non-financial Performance Indicators of BMW Group.
Source: BMW Group's annual report (2014, p. 3)

While financial indicators or monetary indicators such as profit before tax, revenue, EBIT, ROE, ROCE, etc. may be seen in table 3.

BMW Group in figures	2010	2011	2012	2013	2014	Change in %
Principal financial performance indicators						
BMW Group						
Profit before tax — € million	4,853	7,383	7,803	7,893[1]	8,707	10.3
Automotive segment						
Revenues — € million	54,137	63,229	70,208	70,630[1]	75,173	6.4
EBIT margin — % (change in %pts)	8.0	11.8	10.8	9.4	9.6	0.2
RoCE — % (change in %pts)	40.2	77.3	73.7	63.0[1]	61.7	-1.3
Motorcycles segment						
RoCE — % (change in %pts)	18.0	10.2	1.8	16.4	21.8	5.4
Financial Services segment						
RoE — % (change in %pts)	26.1	29.4	21.2	20.0[1]	19.4	-0.6
Further financial key performance figures in € million						
Capital expenditure	3,263	3,692	5,240	6,711[1]	6,100	-9.1
Depreciation and amortisation	3,682	3,646	3,541	3,741[1]	4,170	11.5
Operating cash flow Automotive segment	8,149	8,110	9,167	9,964[1]	9,423	-5.4
Revenues	60,477	68,821	76,848	76,059[1]	80,401	5.7
— Automotive	54,137	63,229	70,208	70,630[1]	75,173	6.4
— Motorcycles	1,304	1,436	1,490	1,504	1,679	11.6
— Financial Services	16,617	17,510	19,550	19,874	20,599	3.6
— Other Entities	4	5	5	6	7	16.7
— Eliminations	-11,585	-13,359	-14,405	-15,955	-17,057	6.9
Profit before financial result (EBIT)	5,111	8,018	8,275	7,978[1]	9,118	14.3
— Automotive	4,355	7,477	7,599	6,649[1]	7,244	8.9
— Motorcycles	71	45	9	79	112	41.8
— Financial Services	1,201	1,763	1,558	1,643	1,756	6.9
— Other Entities	-41	-19	58	44	71	61.4
— Eliminations	-475	-1,248	-949	-437[1]	-65	85.1
Profit before tax	4,853	7,383	7,803	7,893[1]	8,707	10.3
— Automotive	3,887	6,823	7,170	6,561	6,886	5.0
— Motorcycles	65	41	6	76	107	40.8
— Financial Services	1,214	1,790	1,561	1,619[1]	1,723	6.4
— Other Entities	45	-168	3	164	154	-6.1
— Eliminations	-358	-1,103	-937	-527	-163	69.1
Income taxes	-1,610	-2,476	-2,692	-2,564[1]	-2,890	-12.7
Net profit	3,243	4,907	5,111	5,329[1]	5,817	9.2
Earnings per share[2] in €	4.93/4.95	7.45/7.47	7.75/7.77	8.08[1]/8.10[1]	8.83/8.85	9.3/9.3

[1] Prior year figures have been adjusted in accordance with IAS 8, see note 9.
[2] Common/preferred stock. In computing earnings per share of preferred stock, earnings to cover the additional dividend of €0.02 per share of preferred stock are spread over the quarters of the corresponding financial year.

Table 3 – Five Years Summary of Financial Performance Indicators of BMW Group.
Source: BMW Group's annual report (2014, p. 4)

In the following table, BMW Group reported on the principal financial and non-financial performance indicators which are applied as the foundation for managing the BMW Group and its segments. Both of indicators are showed through column charts in figure 12.

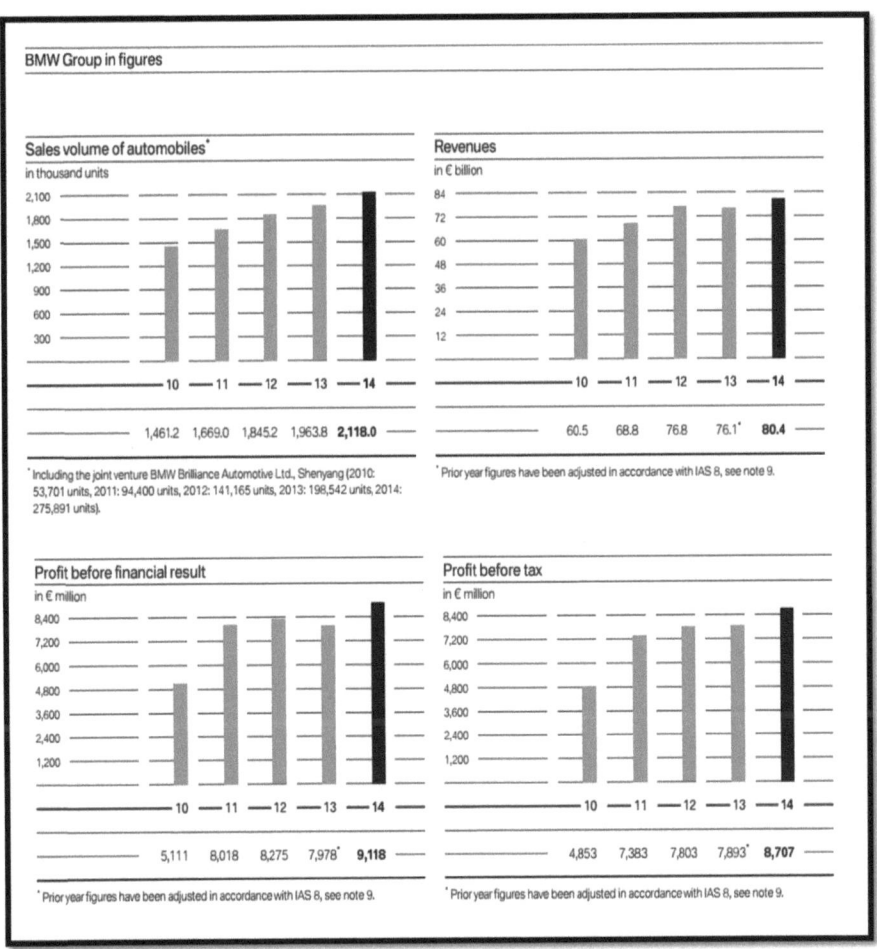

Figure 12 – Five Years Summary of Non-financial and Financial Performance Indicators of BMW Group Showed in Column Charts.
Source: BMW Group's annual report (2014, p. 5)

By comparing at profit before tax in 2014 with the prior year, it should be seen that the BMW group achieved a new record Group profit before tax of €8,707 million. This result represents an increase in the number of vehicles sold.

According to BMW Group's annual report (2014, p. 38), Research and development become an important role for the BMW Group because without them, the high number of new models and its broad range of products would be difficult to be achieved. More than 11,500 employees during 2014 were involved for the BMW Group's global research and innovation network at twelve locations. They spread over five countries to deliver the best product quality possible and develop innovative technologies for customers.

As stated in BMW Group's annual report (2014, p. 44), the BMW Group had employed 116,324 people worldwide at 31 December 2014. The increase of 5.4% from prior year (2013: 110,351 employees) was caused by the expansion of its international production network and the increased scale of development activities to deliver innovations and new technologies for the future. Furthermore, BMW Group provided more apprentices worldwide for young people and invested in employee training. The expenditure on basic and further training rose from €288 million in 2013 to €355 million in 2014, with the main focus of training on electromobility, modern production techniques and healthcare programmes. Moreover, BMW Group believes that "Diversity ensures Competitiveness". In other words, diversity should deliver a major contribution to improving its competitiveness. BMW Group concentrates on three criteria including the respect of gender, the cultural background and the age or experience.

Furthermore, as reported in its annual report (2014, p. 34), BMW Group launched pilot projects for "Industrie 4.0." which would open the way towards the first intelligent plant. The objective is to spread new technologies as sensibly as possible with the purpose of providing production and upstream preparation staff with the best possible support, for example, the innovative collaboration between employee and robots.

According to its annual report (2014, p. 19), BMW group stated that:

> "Our core BMW brand satisfies a broad spectrum of customer wishes, ranging from fuel-efficient, innovative models equipped with Efficient Dynamics through to high-performance, extremely efficient BMW M sub-brand vehicles, which bring the flair of motor sport onto the roads."

This statement shows that BMW's customers were satisfied because BMW sells its products to them and BMW also does not forget to observe what its customers expected from its products. BMW lays customer wishes as an important role for its company's success.

Chapter 4 Analysis of using BSC

4.1. Cause-and-effect correlations

Cause-and-effect correlations should be recognised after we read from our two examples of German companies above, where Daimler AG determined that its goals are technology leadership and innovation, delighted customers, best teams, profitable growth which was targeting to achieve a ROS of 9% (EBIT in relation to revenue) on average for the automotive business. To achieve those goals, the concept of BSC enables to be applied with first placing its financial target of achieving a ROS of 9%, then considering of how the customers should be delighted purchasing its products or services. Daimler improved its services (sales and after sales) and manufactured its futuristic products with inserting future-oriented technologies. However, it should be supported by its innovation and technology which are modern, sophisticated and futuristic, so that its products should be delighted by its customers and automatically increasing sales volume related with increasing Return on Sales (ROS). Moreover, satisfaction of its employees is important due to without well-skilled employees a futuristic high-quality product may not be produced. Therefore, Daimler supports its employees to acquire training programs and further education. If we see on table 1, a series of increasing revenue from 2010 (€97,761 millions) to 2014 (€129,872 millions) as well as operating profit/EBIT from 2010 (€7,274 millions) to 2014 (€10,752 millions) should be seen. It is something which logically may happen, when Daimler AG did not ignore other factors (customers, internal processes and employees). Furthermore, as shown in figure 9 and figure 10 a comparison has been showed that a car product from Daimler AG is safer than a car product from China. As a result, it enables Daimler's customers are satisfied with its products, then, it increases volume of sales, and an increase on revenue may arise.

Analysing at BMW Group's side, where "Strategy Number ONE" was applied and had goals to be profitable and to enhance long-term value in times of change, BMW Group is aware that enhancing long-term value of its company is also important to be a target which should be achieved. To achieve this, BMW Group inserted technological, structural and cultural aspects into its strategy and, in 2007, BMW placed its four pillars which are Growth, Shaping the future, Profitability and Access to Technologies and Customers.

Profitability belongs to financial aspect that every time should be seen through annual reports. However, before obtaining profit, there are other aspects which should not be forgotten and may influence in up and down number of profits such customers aspect. To make its customers satisfied, BMW Group observed what its customers expect. Manufacturing its products for its customers with fuel-efficient, innovative, high-performance models are some examples that BMW pay attention for its customers. However, they consider customers in its production process to make the best product quality and to develop innovative technologies for customer wishes. BMW Group hired more than 11,500 people for the BMW Group's global research and innovation network at twelve locations. Furthermore, BMW Group launched pilot projects for "Industry 4.0" which enabled to support its employees. This pilot project is described as a new technology implementing robots in production processes that may support its employees. Nevertheless, to support a combination between employees and robots, BMW Group did not forget to invest in employee training programmes. Based on BMW Group's annual report (2014, p. 44), from 2013 to 2014, BMW Group increased its investment from €288 million to €355 million by focusing on training on electromobility, modern production techniques and healthcare programmes.

Finally, positive impacts may be seen in table 3. A series of increase of BMW Group's Revenues from 2010 (€60,477 million) to 2014 (€80.401 million) and EBIT from 2010 (€5,111 million) to 2014 (€9,118 million) have been shown. These positive increases certainly were caused from a series of increase of non-financial indicators shown in table 2, where sales volume of BMW Group rose from 95,453 in 2010 to 116,324 in 2014. All of these increases were caused by not only financial aspect but also other aspects.

4.2. Advantages and Disadvantages of BSC

The advantages of BSC as strategic controlling instrument should be seen. Especially, this concept is appropriate for managers to settle their responsibility such as planning, organising, leading and controlling and to enable top managers implement their strategies for real. BSC is able to be used to complete the existing strategy which is usually carried out by Top-managers or CEO. BSC is known as a strategic controlling instrument which is future-oriented and multidimensional because it is based on looking at the entire company and involves not only one aspect (financial related to shareholders) but also other aspects (customers, processes and employees). If it is compared to traditional-oriented Performance Measurement instruments, BSC is more appropriate to the actual demands of the market which are oriented for the future since it is not limited to measuring monetary targets only but also consider non-monetary, however quantitative goals. For example, Daimler AG and BMW Group manufactured vehicles which are futuristic, modern, sophisticated, fuel-efficient, and innovative. Furthermore, BSC provides clarity on organisation's future perspectives and is trustable to deliver an accurate understanding of goals and the methods for attaining goals in complex environments. The "Balanced" should be understood as the balance between short and long-term objectives; past, present and future; financial and non-financial perspectives as well as internal and external perspectives. The concept of BSC has benefits for the top managers who usually have problem to explain their strategies to the end-level and this concept has an ability to translate the idea of CEO on each level. Through this concept, Daimler AG and BMW Group may monitor their current performance (financial, customer satisfaction, and business process results) and their efforts to improve processes, motivate and educate employees through training programmes, and enhance information systems. Since BSC is related with monetary and non-monetary indicators, this concept may be concluded as a complete strategic controlling tool. Furthermore, this concept also contains with early and late indicators, so that it delivers benefits for a company in determining actions should be taken. For examples, with the help of early and late indicators, managers should be informed about error rate, customer satisfaction, customer loyalty, employees' qualification and with the aid of these indicators, Balanced Scorecard is evaluated as a concept leading an objectivity because performance of company's success may be seen through figure, so that an assessment of company's success is more objective. In other words, if a CEO has informed its targets to each low-level manager who has been reinformed this targets to low-level employees, then, in the future, these low-level employees has successfully been operating what low-level manager informed and achieving its targets, the CEO may evaluate its resulted performance with aid of indicators, whether its targets had been achieved or not.

Starting with financial objectives and then connecting them to the customers wishes, internal processes, and finally employees and systems, the concept of BSC is well structured and reasonable. Other benefit offered by BSC is providing important insights into acquisition performance and outcomes because considerations based on the experience of customers, employees, managers and contractors. Furthermore, the usage of four perspectives should be adjusted because different market situations, product strategies and competitive environments require different scorecards.

Nevertheless, this concept should be deemed as an expensive strategic controlling instrument, because it involves four perspectives. Although, Kaplan and Norton (1993) emphasised that a manager should not use four of these perspectives because they should be adjusted by its situations, product strategies and competitive environments. Furthermore, this scorecard (i.g., the four perspectives) should be accurately designed to reflect the corporate strategy, so that goals, investments and activities are connected to the objectives and measures of the scorecard. However, if a company want to use all of these perspectives, this company should prepare a huge budget. In other words, the concept of BSC may be applied only by companies which have huge revenue such as Daimler AG and BMW Group so that they have enough budget to invest more especially in additional coaching or training for employees, upgrading information technology and systems and aligning corporate procedures and routines. Furthermore, a very good co-ordination between top managers and low-level managers as well as employees on each level is very required. CEO should promptly and transparently communicate its vision, mission, strategy map and BSC to all employees on each level. Moreover, in implementing BSC, management from all levels and divisions of company should be intensive involved and the cross-functional team work should be supported by CEO. CEO also should support through providing fund on each needs of its employees. For example, spending fund for employee training programs or for providing sophisticated tools to support each activity of employees.

4.3. Chances and challenges of implementing BSC

If a top manager has a chance to introduce BSC to its employees on each level, he should be ready considering not only one factor but any other factors. However, this concept came for helping manager's tasks in achieving company's objectives and also it may help the manager to translate his idea to the low level managers or to the low-level employees. In implementing BSC, managers are forced to accept the challenges which are not easy. For example, it might be easy for managers to observe one aspect, but now, when they implemented the concept of BSC, they should be forced to consider more than one aspect. Furthermore, to recognise customers wishes is not easy and implementing BSC would require big budget to invest in innovation, research and development, training programmes for employees. For example, BMW Group regards research and development as an important factor for its company's success because without them, the high number of new models would be difficult carried out.

If a manager would try forgetting one aspect, for instance, internal business processes such as research and development for a reason of thrift, a case such as what happened with China's Brilliance BS6 would probably happen. Because of that, a manager should be brave to decide the direction of its company. If a manager decides to bring its company to focus on quality, then, the manager should not forget other perspectives, because each perspective is linked. This may be a challenge for the managers who work with a small company and small budget which usually considers about its profit and quantity without caring other aspects and usually spends low budget on research and development, so that it is very difficult to keep its quality on its products and difficult to fulfil customer wishes which mostly are wishing a modern, sophisticated, futuristic product.

Chapter 5 Conclusion

After we recognised that:
- ➢ The concept of balanced scorecard involves four perspectives (financial, customer, internal business process and learning & growth).
- ➢ It came from an idée that the traditional instruments might not be helpful to measure the company performance because currently a company needs to observe other perspectives to obtain more specific measurement so that information are able to be collected from these perspectives which would help a manager to determine a right decision related to company profits.
- ➢ It was developed by Kaplan & Norton, BSC works with the help of indicators system which is monetary and non-monetary indicators.
- ➢ It had been implemented in two big automobile industries such as Daimler AG and BMW Group and it provides many benefits for them.

Thus, we may summarise that the concept of balanced scorecard should deliver many benefits for top managers or CEO and especially for big companies such as Daimler AG and BMW Group which already indirectly or directly implemented its four perspectives of balanced scorecard in their strategies. Furthermore, this concept offers not only a clarity on organisation's future perspectives but also positive impact on company's revenue or company's EBIT as seen in our two examples of two German companies.

The concept of BSC is concept which is future-oriented and multidimensional because it involves not only one aspect (financial related to shareholders) but also any other aspects (customers, processes and employees). Through this concept, the corporate strategies are operationalised and made measureable with aid of strategic goals, indicators (e.g., Monetary and Non-monetary), annual targets and actions.

With aid of its indicators which are able to make this concept more objective in giving evaluation and which would be connected to the company's main goals, BSC also should appraise performance of company's success. Nevertheless, in its implementation, a company needs to provide budget which is not small especially for research and development.

The result of BSC's success to bring company being more benefits and achieving its targets may be seen in long term period because to conduct research and development, to provide well-trained and well-skilled workers, to see the satisfaction of customers and to see whether with looking at these four perspectives would deliver a positive result in annual report of company are taking time in its process. For example, customers purchased a product, they should evaluate whether this product is sustainable or not, has top quality or not and is sophisticated or not, after he might be seeing in long-term period (e.g., five to ten years).

The most important thing that should be remembered is four perspectives of BSC are linked with each other. The success key of implementing BSC is based on „Balance" in its each perspective. Therefore, if a manager works in a big company which has similarity with BMW AG or Daimler AG, introducing the concept of balanced scorecard is recommended because BSC has been proven helping big companies such as BMW AG and Daimler AG to increase their revenue caused by its more future-oriented, customer-oriented and employee-oriented concept.

In conclusion, it is necessary to insert the concept of BSC in your company because BSC is described as a plausible method to achieve the company's goals. Although the financial perspective is defined as a final objective, it would be connected to the other perspectives through cause-and-effect relations. In addition, currently, it is very necessary to pay attention to other aspects such as customers, internal business process and employees. For example, paying attention to what our customers wish should lead a positive benefit for end result of company's financial aspect. Since the concept of BSC belongs to strategic controlling instrument which is reviewed for period of about one to five years, the positive end result of implementing BSC may not be seen immediately. Nevertheless, it would provide informative, precise, objective and explicit analysis that may be helpful for a manager in taking a right decision. Thus, a focus from the manager to operate this concept properly is very necessary and it is important designing its scorecard accurately to reflect the corporate strategy. As described on help.sap.com (n.d.), a good Balanced Scorecard is designed with three principles (Cause-and-Effect Relationship, Outcomes and Performance Drivers and Connection to Financials) that link the measures to strategy.

List of References

Books:

Asefaso, A., 2013. *Balanced Scorecard.* AA Global Sourcing Ltd.

Bauer, G. 2010. *Strategisches Management in einer Autobank mit der Balanced Scorecard – So setzt BMW Group Financial Services die Unternehmensstrategie in einer globalen Organisation erfolgreich um.* In: Stenner, F. (Ed.) 2015: Handbuch Automobilbanken - Finanzdienstleistungen für Mobilität. Berlin: Springer-Verlag. pp. 433-443.

Disselkamp, M., Schüller R., 2004. *Lieferantenrating - Instrumente, Kriterien, Checklisten.* Wiesbaden: Springer.

Erichsen, J., 2011. *Controlling-Instrumente von A–Z: Die wichtigsten Werkzeuge zur Unternehmenssteuerung.* 8th ed. München: Rudolf Haufe.

Gabriel, A., 2004. *Ausgestaltung einer Balanced Scorecard für Versicherungsunternehmen* (Vol. 49). Karlsruhe: Versicherungswirtschaft.

Hirt, M. (Ed.), 2015. *Die wichtigsten Strategietools für Manager – Mehr Orientierung für den Unternehmenserfolg.* München: Vahlen.

Jahnke, B., Sassmann, T., 2003. Leadership-oriented Executive Information Systems. In: Berndt, R., 2003: *Leadership in turbulenten Zeiten.* Berlin: Springer-Verlag. p. 344.

Kaplan, R. S., & Norton, D. P., 1996. *The balanced scorecard: translating strategy into action.* USA: Harvard Business Press.

Lewis, P.S., Goodman, S.H., Fandt, P.M., Michlitsch, J.F., 2007. *Management - challenges for Tomorrow's Leaders.* 5th ed. USA: Thomson Learning.

Lohrmann, M., Reichert, M., 2013. Understanding Business Process Quality. In: Glykas, M. (Ed.), *Business Process Management: Theory and Applications.* Berlin: Springer.

Schermerhorn, J.R., 2011. *Management.* 11th ed. USA: John Wiley & Sons.

Schmeisser, W., Clausen, L., Popp, R., Ennemann, C., Drewicke, O., 2011. *Controlling and Berlin Balanced Scorecard Approach.* München: Oldenbourgh.

Schmeisser, W., Claussen, L., 2009. *Controlling und Berliner Balanced Scorecard Ansatz.* München: Oldenbourg Verlag.

Sherwood, J., Clark, A., Lynas, D., 2005. *Enterprise Security Architecture: A Business-Driven Approach.* Boca Raton (USA): CRC Press.

Taguchi, Y., Kaneko, T., Tabe, T., 2009. *A Method for Evaluation the Relationship Four Perspectives of the Balanced Scorecard.* In: Smith, M.J., Slavendy, G. (Eds.), 2009. Human Interface and the Management of Information. Designing Information Environments. Berlin: Springer.

Von der Gathen, A., 2014. *Das große Handbuch der Strategieinstrumente - Werkzeuge für eine erfolgreiche Unternehmensführung.* 3th ed. Frankfurt: Campus Verlag.

Weber, J., Schäffer, U., 2008. *Introduction to Controlling.* Stuttgart: Schäffer-Poeschel.

Internet:

ADAC.com, n.d. *Crash-Tests - Mercedes C-Klasse (Modell ab 2014).* [internet] Available at: <https://www.adac.de/infotestrat/tests/crash-test/detail.aspx?IDtest=447> [Accessed 1 November 2015].

Autobild.de, 2007. *ADAC-CRASHTEST BRILLIANCE BS6: Schrott aus China.* [internet] Available at: <http://www.autobild.de/artikel/adac-crashtest-brilliance-bs6-220767.html> [Accessed 15.11.2015].

Averson, P., 1998. *Background and History of Measurement-Based Management.* [internet] Available at: balancedscorecard.org website <https://balancedscorecard.org/Resources/Articles-White-Papers/Background> [Accessed 29 July 2015].

Balancedscorecard.org, n.d. *Balanced Scorecard Adopters.* [internet] Available at: < https://balancedscorecard.org/Resources/About-the-Balanced-Scorecard/Balanced-Scorecard-Adopters> [Accessed 19 October 2015].

Bmwgroup.com, 2008. *Sustainability Management.* [internet] Available at: <http://www.bmwgroup.com/e/0_0_www_bmwgroup_com/verantwortung/publikationen/sustainable_value_report_2008/_pdf/SVR_2008_engl_Kapitel_1.pdf> [Accessed 19 October 2015].

Bmwgroup.com, 2014. *Annual Report 2014.* [internet] Available at: < http://www.bmwgroup.com/e/0_0_www_bmwgroup_com/investor_relations/corporate_events/hauptversammlung/2015/_pdf/12507_GB_2014_en_Finanzbericht_Online.pdf> [Accessed 19 October 2015].

Bmwgroup.com, n.d. *Services - Glossary.* [internet] Available at: < http://www.bmwgroup.com/e/0_0_www_bmwgroup_com/verantwortung/services/glossar.html#6> [Accessed 19 October 2015].

Bmwgroup.com, n.d., *Company Portrait – Business Segments.* [internet] Available at: < http://www.bmwgroup.com/bmwgroup_prod/e/0_0_www_bmwgroup_com/unternehmen/unternehmensprofil/geschaeftsbereiche/geschaeftsbereiche.html > [Accessed 15 November 2015].

Bmwgroup.com, n.d., Company Portrait - *Strategy.* [internet] Available at: < http://www.bmwgroup.com/bmwgroup_prod/e/0_0_www_bmwgroup_com/unternehmen/unternehmensprofil/strategie/strategie.html > [Accessed 15 November 2015].

Bmwgroup.com, n.d., *Company.* [internet] Available at: < http://www.bmwgroup.com/bmwgroup_prod/com/en/company/index.html> [Accessed 19 October 2015].

Bmwgroup.com, n.d., *Corporate facts – Board of Management.* [internet] Available at: < http://www.bmwgroup.com/bmwgroup_prod/e/0_0_www_bmwgroup_com/unternehmen/unternehmensprofil/vorstand/vorstand.html> [Accessed 19 October 2015].

Daimler.com, 2009. *Jahresfinanzbericht 2009.* [internet] Available at: < http://www.cms.daimler.com/Projects/c2c/channel/documents/1813938_DAI_2009_Jahresfinanzbericht.pdf> [Accessed 15 October 2015].

Daimler.com, 2011. *Sustainability Report 2011.* [internet] Available at: < http://www.cms.daimler.com/Projects/c2c/channel/documents/2313176_Daimler_Sustainability_Report_2011.pdf> [Accessed 15 October 2015].

Daimler.com, 2014. *Annual Report 2014.* [internet] Available at: < http://www.cms.daimler.com/Projects/c2c/channel/documents/2590177_Daimler_FY_2014_Annual_Financial_Report.pdf> [Accessed 14 October 2015].

Daimler.com, 2014. *Sustainability Report 2014.* [internet] Available at: <http://www.cms.daimler.com/Projects/c2c/channel/documents/2621687_Daimler_Sustainability_Report_2014_EN.pdf> [Accessed 14 October 2015].

Daimler.com, n.d., *Company.* [internet] Available at: <https://www.daimler.com/company> [Accessed 14 October 2015].

Daimler.com, n.d., *Our Brands.* [internet] Available at: <https://www.daimler.com/brands-and-products/our-brands> [Accessed 1 November 2015].

Haufe.de, n.d. Kennzahlen/2 Arten von Kennzahlen. [internet] Available at: <http://www.haufe.de/unternehmensfuehrung/profirma-professional/kennzahlen-2-arten-von-kennzahlen_idesk_PI11444_HI6649337.html> [Accessed 13.10.2015].

help.sap.com, n.d. *Creating Strategic Focus: The Balanced Scorecard.* [internet] Available at: <http://help.sap.com/saphelp_erp60_sp/helpdata/en/88/9fcf535b804808e10000000a174cb4/content.htm> [Accessed 09.10.2015].

Kaplan, R. S., Norton. D. P., 1993. *Putting the Balanced Scorecard to Work.* [Online] Available at: Harvard Business Review <https://hbr.org/1993/09/putting-the-balanced-scorecard-to-work> [Accessed: 09.10.2015].

Kaplan, R.S., Norton, D.P., 2005. The *Balanced Scorecard: Measures that Drive Performance.* [Online] Available at: Harvard Business Review <https://hbr.org/2005/07/the-balanced-scorecard-measures-that-drive-performance> [Accessed 28 July 2015].

Lehr, T., 2010. *Die Balanced-Scorecard zur Strategieentwicklung für Startups.* [Online] Available at: Gründerszene.de Website <http://www.gruenderszene.de/allgemein/die-balanced-scorecard-zur-strategieentwicklung-fur-startups> [Accessed 29 July 2015].

Prnewswire.com, 2004. *Chrysler Group Named to the Balanced Scorecard Hall of Fame.* [internet] Available at: <http://www.prnewswire.com/news-releases/chrysler-group-named-to-the-balanced-scorecard-hall-of-fame-74293507.html> [Accessed 14 October 2015].

Procurement Executives' Association, 1998. *Guide to a balanced scorecard: performance management methodology - moving from performance measurement to performance management.* [internet] suub.uni-bremen.de, Available at: <http://suche.suub.uni-bremen.de/peid=ftumichgbhathioaiquodlibumichedumiu01003322769&LAN=DE&CID=4383924&index=L&Hitnr=6> [Accessed: 10.08.2015].

Savkin, A., 2011. *Your guide to Balanced Scorecard - from motivation to implementation.* [internet], Available at: <https://books.google.de/books?id=pXCHAwAAQBAJ&printsec=frontcover&hl=de#v=onepage&q&f=false> [Accessed: 8.10.2015].

Tham, E., 2013. *Stuck in First Gear: Chinese Car Manufacturers Struggle to compete with foreign brands.* [internet] Available at: CKGSB Knowledge <http://knowledge.ckgsb.edu.cn/2013/07/30/china/chinese-car-manufacturers-struggle-to-compete-with-foreign-brands/> [Accessed 02.11.2015].

Uk.reuters.com, 2007. *Another Chinese car flunks German crash test.* [internet] Available at: <http://uk.reuters.com/article/2007/06/22/chinese-crash-test-idUKNOA23009720070622> [Accessed 02.11.2015].

Journals:

Grove, H., Cook, T., Richter, K., 2008. Coors Balanced Scorecard: a decade of experience. *IMA Educational Case Journal.* [e-journal] 1(1). Available at: <http://www.imanet.org/docs/default-source/academic/iecj_coors_cs.pdf?sfvrsn=2> [Accessed 13 October 2015].

Mooraj, S., Oyon, D., Hostettler, D., 1999. The Balanced Scorecard: a Necessary Good or an Unnecessary Evil?. *European Management Journal.* [e-journal] 17(5). Available at:<http://ac.els-cdn.com/S0263237399000341/1-s2.0-S0263237399000341-main.pdf?_tid=6aefee62-7016-11e5-a355-00000aab0f6c&acdnat=1444567909_fe70519aab8de53ee9f3c03e18246917> [Accessed 11 October 2015].

Poureisa, A., Ahmadgourabi, M. B. A., & Efteghar, A., 2013. Balanced Scorecard: A New Tool for Performance Evaluation. *Interdisciplinary Journal of Contemporary Research In Business.* [e-journal] 5(1). Available at:<http://journal-archieves32.webs.com/974-978.pdf> [Accessed 30 July 2015].

TESAROVIČOVÁ, I., 2008. Modern Approaches to Leading an Organization with focus on Human Capital. *Journal of Information, Control and Management Systems.* [e-journal] 6(2). Available at:<http://kifri.fri.uniza.sk/ojs/index.php/JICMS/article/viewFile/1016/395> [Accessed 30 July 2015].

Figures:

ADAC.com, n.d. *Crash-Tests - Mercedes C-Klasse (Modell ab 2014).* [internet] Available at: <https://www.adac.de/infotestrat/tests/crash-test/detail.aspx?IDtest=447> [Accessed 1 November 2015].

Autobild.de, 2007. *ADAC-CRASHTEST BRILLIANCE BS6: Schrott aus China.* [internet] Available at: <http://www.autobild.de/artikel/adac-crashtest-brilliance-bs6-220767.html> [Accessed 15.11.2015].

Bmwgroup.com, 2014. *Annual Report 2014.* [internet] Available at: < http://www.bmwgroup.com/e/0_0_www_bmwgroup_com/investor_relations/corporate_events/hauptversammlung/2015/_pdf/12507_GB_2014_en_Finanzbericht_Online.pdf> [Accessed 19 October 2015].

Bmwgroup.com, 2015. *Corporate Facts: Board of Management.* [internet] Available at: < http://www.bmwgroup.com/bmwgroup_prod/e/0_0_www_bmwgroup_com/unternehmen/unternehmensprofil/vorstand/vorstand.html> [Accessed 15 November 2015].

Business-process-it.com, 2008. *Balanced Scorecard (BSC): How strong is your Business Tree ?.* [internet] Available at: < http://www.business-process-it.com/balanced-scorecard.html> [Accessed 15 November 2015].

Daimler.com, 2014. *Annual Report 2014.* [internet] Available at: < http://www.cms.daimler.com/Projects/c2c/channel/documents/2590177_Daimler_FY_2014_Annual_Financial_Report.pdf> [Accessed 14 October 2015].

Daimler.com, 2015. *Board of Management.* [internet] Available at: < https://www.daimler.com/dccom/0-5-65183-1-65184-1-0-0-0-0-0-135-7145-0-0-0-0-0-0-0.html> [Accessed 15 November 2015].

Haufe.de, n.d. *Kennzahlen/2 Arten von Kennzahlen.* [internet] Available at: <http://www.haufe.de/unternehmensfuehrung/profirma-professional/kennzahlen-2-arten-von-kennzahlen_idesk_PI11444_HI6649337.html> [Accessed 13.10.2015].

Lewis, P.S., Goodman, S.H., Fandt, P.M., Michlitsch, J.F., 2007. *Management - challenges for Tomorrow's Leaders.* 5th ed. USA: Thomson Learning.

Nafatni, K., 2012. *Sunrise in the office.* [Online] Available at: <https://500px.com/photo/33047399/sunrise-in-the-office-by-karim-nafatni?from=user> [Accessed 7.10.2015].

Procurement Executives' Association, 1998. *Guide to a balanced scorecard : performance management methodology* - moving from performance measurement to performance management. [internet] suub.uni-bremen.de, Available at: <http://suche.suub.uni-bremen.de/peid=ftumichgbhathioaiquodlibumichedumiu01003322769&LAN=DE&CID=4383924&index=L&Hitnr=6> [Accessed: 10.08.2015].

Tables:

Bmwgroup.com, 2014. *Annual Report 2014.* [internet] Available at: < http://www.bmwgroup.com/e/0_0_www_bmwgroup_com/investor_relations/corporate_events/hauptversammlung/2015/_pdf/12507_GB_2014_en_Finanzbericht_Online.pdf> [Accessed 19 October 2015].

Daimler.com, 2014. *Annual Report 2014.* [internet] Available at: < http://www.cms.daimler.com/Projects/c2c/channel/documents/2590177_Daimler_FY_2014_Annual_Financial_Report.pdf> [Accessed 14 October 2015].